THINGS TO DO IN GRAND RAPIDS BEFORE YOU DIE

Sculpture in front of Blue Bridge.
Photo credit: Christine Nyholm

100 THINGS TO DO IN GRAND RAPIDS BEFORE YOU DIE

NORMA LEWIS AND CHRISTINE NYHOLM

Reedy Press
PO Box 5131
St. Louis, MO 63139, USA
www.reedypress.com

Library of Congress Control Number: 2018962614

ISBN: 9781681062013

Design by Jill Halpin

Printed in the United States of America
19 20 21 22 23 5 4 3 2 1

Please note that websites, phone numbers, addresses, and company names are subject to change or cancellation. We did our best to relay the most accurate information available, but due to circumstances beyond our control, please do not hold us liable for misinformation. When exploring new destinations, please do your homework before you go.

DEDICATION

For Fay Reilly
N. L.

In loving memory of my parents, Norman and Lydia Bude
C. N.

• •

John Ball Zoo celebrates Halloween.
Photo credit: Christine Nyholm

CONTENTS

Music and Entertainment

Sports and Recreation

Culture and History

Shopping and Fashion

PREFACE

Grand Rapids is Michigan's second largest city, 168 miles and a world away from Detroit, the largest. The city and surrounding suburbs have a population of around 200,000. Native Americans lived here first, and French Canadian voyageurs established trading posts in the area in the nineteenth century. Like most cities of its size, Grand Rapids has reinvented itself over the years. The Grand River and abundant forests throughout the state fueled the lumber industry. That led to the city enjoying a century-long reign as "Furniture City." Today we're Beer City, and our Medical Mile places us on the cutting edge of the health care industry.

A job brought me here in 1972. I lived and worked in the suburb of Wyoming, and have observed many changes in the years since. Industry declined, replaced by health care, education, and tourism. And let's not forget the beer! Through it all, Grand Rapids has remained a vibrant community where residents view their hometown with pride.

—Norma Lewis

ACKNOWLEDGMENTS

Compiling a guidebook requires assistance from many sources. A big thank you to the owners of some of the businesses featured, not only for your input but also for your enthusiasm for this project. It is people like you who make a city great. We hope you will be pleased with the end result. Thanks also to the Grand Rapids Public Museum, Shops at MoDiv, and the West Michigan Whitecaps for providing images.

Working with the Reedy Press team has been a great pleasure! Josh Stevens, Barbara Northcott, Don Korte, Mischelle Marlow-Leahy, Mary Beth Stevens, and Quin McIntosh, you're the best. Your hands-on attention to detail throughout the process is very much appreciated.

As always, we are indebted to our families and friends for their ongoing encouragement.

We're also indebted to Janet Korn and Stephanie Kotschevar at Experience Grand Rapids. Thank you for meeting with us and for your excellent suggestions. Your organization is doing a terrific job of making people aware of the great city on the Grand and all it has to offer.

Brewery Vivant decorated for Halloween.
Photo credit: Christine Nyholm

FOOD AND DRINK

ENJOY
FINE DINING

The Chop House, an atmospheric restaurant decorated with gaslight, is one of the city's most popular special occasion restaurants. Fans of great food and fine wine and cocktails dine at the steak house for the Midwestern USDA Prime beef and premium seafood, located across from the Amway Grand Plaza Hotel.

The Chop House, 190 Monroe Ave. NW
thechophousegrandrapids.com

Palio, 545 Michigan NE, Ste. 102
paliograndrapids.com

(888) 456-3463 (DINE)

TIP

Looking to celebrate a birthday? Check out the birthday specials at the Chop House or Palio and receive a substantial discount on food. The discount is 50 percent off for a party of two and slides down for larger parties. The birthday dinner must be on the actual date of your birthday and official ID will be required to verify the birthday. Happy birthday!

2

BON APPETIT
AT SIX.ONE.SIX RESTAURANT

Enjoy fine, French-inspired cuisine at six.one.six, located in the lobby of the J. W. Marriott Hotel in downtown Grand Rapids. Named for the Grand Rapids area code, they are dedicated to sustainable practices, buying and serving food made from local ingredients and serving Michigan-made craft beers and wines. You can enjoy elegant but casual dining for breakfast, lunch, and dinner. Bon appétit!

235 Louis Campau Stl. NW, (616) 242-1448
ilovetheJW.com

3

HAVE FRIENDS WITH BENEDICTS
AT THE CHERIE INN

The Cherie Inn is located where Cherry, Diamond, and Lake streets intersect in the trendy East Hills area. Open since 1924, it is the longest-running restaurant in the city. The hundred-year-old building itself adds to the ambience, with the original tin ceilings and Grand Rapids–made Stickley furnishings dating from the 1940s and the city's prominence in the furniture industry.

But people don't patronize restaurants for ambience as much as for food, and the Cherie excels in that area too. It serves only breakfast and lunch and signature dishes keep a satisfied clientele coming back for more. Among breakfast favorites are a selection of "Benedicts" that, along with traditional Eggs Benedict, include Crab Cakes Benedict, Grilled Steak Benedict, and Avocado Benedict. Lunch selections include an array of sandwiches, including a popular vegetarian option made of sautéed mushrooms, broccoli, carrots, and tomatoes with herbed cream cheese and grilled to perfection on seven-grain bread. Soups change seasonally and in colder months include cream of portabella mushroom. No detail is too small here, from the fresh flowers to servers who are attentive but never hover.

969 Cherry St. SE, (616) 458-0588
cherieinn.com

MAKE FRIENDS
WITH BOB (B.O.B.)

The Big Old Building has it all: dining, entertainment, and a lounge. The Gilmore Group operates them all and is headquartered in the building. Is your dinner a special occasion? You can't go wrong with the steaks at Judson's, or if you prefer seafood, stop in at Gilly's, both for the oyster bar and the seafood menu. For casual fare there's Bobarino's wood-fired pizzas and dueling pianos, or the B.O.B.'s brewery for handcrafted beer. It really is a big old building because there's also room for H.O.M.E. (House of Music and Entertainment), along with Dr. Grin's Comedy Club. Or stop in at the end of an evening on the town for a nightcap and a spin around the dance floor at Eve, the late-night lounge. Located just steps away from the Van Andel Arena, it's a great spot to stop before or after attending a game.

20 Monroe Ave. NW, (616) 356-2000
thebob.com

5

TOUR FOUNDERS BREWING
AND HOIST SOME BREWS

Grand Rapids proudly calls itself "Beer City," and Founders Brewery is considered the most popular brewery in the city. Visit Founders to tour the brewery, walk the catwalk and learn about the craft of beer making and the history of the brewery. You can also taste some of their beers, such as All Day IPA, Dirty Bastard, Centennial IPA, and Solid Gold.

The taproom, which overlooks the brewhouse, is modeled after a German beer hall and is complete with a patio and beer garden. Enjoy a handcrafted sandwich along with your beer of choice.

Tours are for adults aged 21+, so ID will be required. You can make reservations and see the tour fee details on the Founders website.

235 Grandville Ave. SW, (616) 776-2182
foundersbrewing.com

TIP

Founders Beers are often available in restaurants, bars, and liquor stores throughout the area, so in addition to drinking them in the taproom, you can enjoy them while out with friends or while relaxing at home. The Mothership Series brews, however, are available only in the taproom locations. The beers could be "oldies but goodies" temporarily taken out of retirement, or experimental new styles. When you visit Founders, be sure to taste beers available from the Mothership Series.

6

HAVE A BURGER
AT THE COTTAGE BAR AND RESTAURANT

You won't be sorry, as *USA Today* voted it Michigan's best burger. Have it with a side of chili, also award-winning. This historic eatery opened in 1927 during Prohibition. No, it wasn't a speakeasy, so the owner drew clientele with card games and other fun activities. The "bar" in its name wasn't added until 1933 when it received a license to serve beer and wine. Displayed in a frame on the wall is one of the first city-issued liquor licenses. It's the kind of place that serves as a sort of melting pot of locals where theatergoers, college students, downtown dwellers, and even church choirs stop in to raise a glass and enjoy the signature burgers.

18 LaGrave Ave. SE, (616) 454-9088
cottagebar.biz

TIP

For another great burger experience, check out the Choo Choo Grill. "Cozy" best describes this space-challenged, train-themed eatery that claims to have "the best burgers on earth or anywhere else."

1209 Plainfield Ave. SE, (616) 774-8652
choochoogrill.weebly.com

7

DRINK FARMHOUSE ALES IN A FORMER CHAPEL
AT BREWERY VIVANT

Brewery Vivant serves farmhouse ales and European food inspired by the small breweries that dot the countryside of southern Belgium and northern France. Enjoy the ambience of the refurbished chapel of a funeral home, with a lofty ceiling and stained-glass windows casting a golden glow on the bar. Patrons sit in booths or at long tables, enjoying camaraderie while relishing tasty food and drink.

The environmentally friendly brewery was awarded a LEEDS certification in 2012, the first ever such award for a production brewery. The management takes pride in their sustainable practices and uses locally sourced ingredients in their food and beverages. This is a must stop for socially conscious lovers of farmhouse ale and European food.

925 Cherry St. SE, (616) 719-1604
breweryvivant.com

TIP

Brewery Vivant is not the only Beer City brewery in a historic building. Check out some of the other breweries that serve food and drinks in an interesting and fun-filled atmosphere.

Harmony Hall is a brewery inside an old sausage factory in Eastown. Mitten Brewing Company is located in a historic firehouse, Engine House No. 9, which dates back to 1890. Creston Brewery is in the old DeKorne Furniture showroom, with natural light shining through floor-to-ceiling windows.

Harmony Hall

401 Stocking Ave. NW, (616) 233-9186
harmonybeer.com

Mitten Brewing Company

527 Leonard St. NW, (616) 608-5612
mittenbrewing.com

Creston Brewery

1504 Plainfield Ave. NE, (616) 805-4523
crestonbrewery.com

8

HAVE A DONUT WITH MARGE

Marge's Donut Den has been a fixture on 28th Street in Wyoming since 1975. Marge Wilson saw a need and filled it through hard work and truly caring about her clientele. She stays open on Christmas Day so that anyone with nowhere else to go will find an open door and a welcoming friend. Friendship is what the shop is all about, from the sign reading "Where Old Friends Meet and Make New Friends" to the tables where people gather to chat and catch up with one another. Along with a tantalizing array of donuts, crullers, muffins, pastries, turnovers, cupcakes, and more, Marge's talented bakers make wedding cakes, groom's cakes, birthday and other celebration cakes, and also create a cake of the month. Marge has been known to host a wedding or two.

1751 28th St. SW, Wyoming, (616) 532-7413
margesdonutden.com

TIP

Prefer staying near downtown? Van's has been around even longer than Marge's, and, as you might expect with a name like Van, you'll find it full of great Dutch treats still made from recipes that third-generation owner John VanderMeer inherited from his grandfather, who brought them with him when he emigrated from the Netherlands.

955 Fulton St. SE, (616) 458-1637

GO CHINESE
AT THE BLUE GINGER ASIAN KITCHEN

The go-to for many Chinese food aficionados, this restaurant bills itself as "a family owned restaurant specializing in made-to-order Chinese American food." You'll also find a few Thai and Vietnamese choices on the menu. The service is impeccable, the staff friendly, the food delicious, and the prices affordable. Chances are the owner will visit your table to make sure everything is to your liking. He'll also make sure you get extra rice when you ask for a box. Perennial favorites are General Tso's, Orange Chicken, Curry Pad Thai, Dragon and Phoenix, and Sweet and Sour Chicken or Shrimp. Spiciness is measured mild, sunny, warm, or heat wave.

5751 Byron Center Ave. SW, Wyoming, (616) 261-8186
bluegingerkitchen.com

TIP

There are numerous Asian restaurants in the area. A favorite of sushi lovers is Sushi Kuni, where the owners offer both traditional and Asian fusion options, including sushi rolls and Bento boxes. Looking for Thai? Look no further than Thai Express.

Sushi Kuni, 2901 Breton Ave. SE, (616) 241-4141
sushikuni.com

Thai Express, 4313 Kalamazoo Ave. SE, Kentwood, (616) 827-9955
thaiexpress.com

10

HOP ON AND OFF
THE BEER TROLLEY

Breweries are plentiful in Beer City U.S.A., so the Beer Trolley gives beer lovers a chance to visit breweries without having to drive between breweries or worry about parking. This is a great way to gather with friends and enjoy a pub day so you can taste the variety of ales and lagers produced by the craft brewers of Grand Rapids.

The Hop On Hop Off Tour stops at each brewery about once an hour. In addition, the breweries offer food, so order some pub food, burgers, or pizza to enjoy with your drinks. Keep in mind that you will still need to get home, so plan for a ride or designated driver and be safe.

The Beer Trolley also runs other tours, including the Fall Color Tour for cider lovers, ArtPrize Tour, and the Christmas Lights Tour. They can also be booked for custom tours, bachelor and bachelorette parties, birthday parties, retirement parties, galas, and more.

861 Emerald Ave., (616) 439-4677
grbeertrolley.com

TIP

If you want to check out additional breweries in Grand Rapids and the surrounding area, check out the Beer City Ale Trail map put out by Experience Grand Rapids. Pick up a brochure along the trail or look it up online at experiencegrandrapids.com/beer.

BREWERIES ON THE HOP ON HOP OFF TOUR

Founders Brewing

235 Grandville Ave. SW, (616) 776-2182
foundersbrewing.com

HopCat

25 Ionia Ave. SW, (616) 451-4677
hopcat.com

Atwater

201 Michigan St. NW, (616) 649-3120
atwater.com

New Holland Knickerbocker

417 Bridge St. NW, (616) 345-5642
newhollandbrew.com

Harmony Hall

401 Stocking Ave. NW, (616) 233-9186
harmonybeer.com

Mitten Brewing Company

527 Leonard St. NW, (616) 608-5612
mittenbrewing.com

City Built

820 Monroe Ave., Ste. 155, (616) 805-5755
citybuiltbrewing.com

B.O.B.'s Brewery

20 Monroe Ave. NW, (616) 356-2000
thebobsbrewery.thebob.com

Grand Rapids Brewing Co.

1 Ionia Ave. SW, (616) 458-7000
grbrewingcompany,com

11

ENJOY A RED HOT
AT THE GRAND CONEY

Burgers may have replaced hot dogs as America's hot sandwich of first choice, but there are still times when nothing but a dog will do. The best of course are those we remember from childhood when we stuck the dog on an unbent coat hanger or stick and roasted it over an open fire. For the next best, head to the Grand Coney diner in Grand Rapids or suburban Allendale. Choose Detroit- or Flint-style Coney dogs or custom order. For some, hot dogs are the best reason to stop in, but they aren't the only one. The Grand Coney breakfast menu offers everything from skillets to omelets to breakfast burritos. This eatery more than lives up to the unofficial diner standard of excellence: good food, friendly staff, and moderate pricing. Find all kinds of sandwiches, salads, soups, and dinners of great diner fare, including meat loaf, fish and chips, and pot roast. The kind of food Mom makes, but give her a day off and bring her here.

TIP

For another hot dog experience, try the Corner Bar in Rockford. Though destroyed by fire in mid-2018, it is once again up and running. And yes, the World Famous Wall of Fame is still there. For the uninitiated, that refers to the names on the wall of all who have earned that privilege by downing a dozen dogs in one sitting.

Also, check out Yesterdog on Wealthy Street in the Eastown neighborhood. It's worth going in to see the 1930s and '40s décor. The dogs are good too.

12

EAT OUT
DURING RESTAURANT WEEK GRAND RAPIDS

Expand your culinary horizons by dining at some restaurants you might not have tried by eating out during Restaurant Week GR. Area restaurants offer special menus during this week in August, so you can dine out at places you have not tried yet. Taste the city with specially priced lunches and dinners during a week in August.

This delectable foodie event features special menus at about seventy-five area restaurants, including craft breweries, ethnic restaurants, sandwich spots, seafood joints, steakhouses, bistros, sports grills, fine dining places, and all the types of eateries in a great foodie city. The special menus are priced to be affordable, so try as many as you can and you just might find a new favorite for repeat visits.

In addition to offering great food specials, Restaurant Week GR donates to a scholarship fund for the Grand Rapids Community College's Secchia Institute for Culinary Education, which educates students in the culinary arts.

Participating restaurants are located in the Greater Grand Rapids area. See the Experience Grand Rapids website for information about participating locations as the special week-long event approaches.

experiencegr.com/restaurant-week

DRINK MEAD
AT ARTKOS

Mead is a sweet nectar made of fermented honey and water that has been enjoyed by cultures for over 9,000 years and is thought to be the oldest alcoholic drink in the world. Mead has been enjoyed by the ancient Greeks, Romans, Vikings, Celts, and more and is still enjoyed today.

You can taste various flavors of mead at Artkos Meadery, a cozy pub with a friendly atmosphere. The mead at Artkos is made from natural wildflower honey from Michigan and Michigan fruits, so it is a local beverage. Queen Bee, a traditional mead, is a tasty sweet nectar to warm and soothe you. The fruit-flavored meads, called melomels, are infused with blueberries, raspberries, black raspberries, strawberries, and more. Artkos specializes in mead and has created several flavors so you can taste the variety of flavors right in Grand Rapids.

1251 Century Ave. SW, (616) 406-4444
artkosmeadery.com

TIP

Mead can also be found at some of the other wineries and distilleries around Grand Rapids, including the following:

Thornapple Brewing Company

6262 28th St., (616) 288-6907
thornapplebrewing.com

Cascade Winery

4665 Broadmoor Ave. SE, Ste. 135, Kentwood, (616) 656-4665
cascadecellars.com

Bardic Wells Meadery

8844 Water St., Montague, (616) 837-8035
bardicwells.com

14

SINK YOUR TEETH
INTO THE BEST PIZZA IN TOWN

Everyone has an opinion of what makes a pizza great, as well as where to find it. For many, that means Vitales, a Grand Rapids fixture for more than fifty years. What started as Salvatore Vitale's shop on Leonard Street has grown into a local chain with restaurants throughout the city and suburbs. The menu has expanded throughout the years and now offers a full range of Italian cuisine. It is still family run and still serves up great food in a convivial sports bar atmosphere. Bring the kids to enjoy the on-site games. Check the website for a list of locations.

If you crave authentic Sicilian pizza, head for Knapp's Corner and Lucari's Sicilian Pizza Kitchen, owned by Gianni and Lisa Lucari. Gianni wanted others to enjoy the food he grew up eating. The secret, according to the Lucari family, is fresh, high-quality ingredients. They have a second shop in suburban Hudsonville.

Since pizza and beer are a perfect pair, it stands to reason that a brewery might serve some of the best pizza around. For wood-fired, locally sourced ingredients, and old favorites with a new twist, try the Harmony Brewing Company in Eastown.

Vitales, 834 Leonard St. NE, (616) 458-8368
vitalespizza.com

Lucari's Sicilian Pizza Kitchen, 2869 Knapp St., (616) 608-6912
lucarispizzakitchen.com

Harmony Brewing Company, 1551 Lake Dr. SE, (616) 233-0063
harmonybeer.com

TASTE MICHIGAN WINES
AT LOCAL WINERIES

Visit a local winery to taste some of the vintages produced from Michigan's famed fruits. Take the time to taste the various vintages, including red, white, sweet, dry, dessert, or fruity wines. There will be a wine for you.

Wine is known as "the fruit of the grape," but there are also wines made from the fine fruits of Michigan, such as blueberry, raspberry, and strawberry. Try some out and discover the variety of flavors to please the senses.

Cascade Cellars Winery, 4665 Broadmoor Ave. SE, Ste. 135, Kentwood
(616) 656-4665
cascadecellars.com

Robinette's Apple Haus & Winery, 3142 4 Mile Rd. NE
(616) 351-5567
robinettes.com

Hudsonville Winery and Pike 51 Brewing, 3768 Chicago Dr., Hudsonville
(616) 662-4589
hudsonvillewinery.com

Bier Distillery, 5295 West River Dr. NE, Ste. 100, Comstock Park
(616) 888-9746
bierdistillery.com

DRINK HARD CIDER
AT A CIDERY

Cideries produce hard cider made from apples and other fruits, which are crushed and fermented. The crops of quality apples around Grand Rapids make the area a natural for cider production. Michigan is a major apple producer in the United States, and more than half of all Michigan apples are grown on Fruit Ridge, about ten minutes north of Grand Rapids.

Vander Mill is a leader in the cider scene, offering a wide selection of ciders, from traditional to flavored, and from sweet to dry. They recently opened a 55,000-square-foot location that includes a tasting room, restaurant, and production facility. You can also experience their food and cider at their facility in Spring Lake.

Vander Mill Grand Rapids offers production tours so you can see how the magic is made and taste some of their tasty ciders. Check their website for the schedule and fee information.

Vander Mill, 505 Ball Ave. NE, (616) 259-8828
vandermill.com

Vander Mill, 14921 Cleveland St., Spring Lake, (616) 842-4337
vandermill.com

CIDERIES

Farmhouse Cider

5025 Stanton St., Hudsonville, (616) 920-1867
farmhouscider.com

Ridge Cider Co.

351 W. 135th St., Grant, (231) 674-2040
ridgecider.com

Robinette's Apple Haus & Winery

3142 4 Mile Rd. NE, (616) 351-5567
robinettes.com

The Peoples Cider Co.

539 Leonard St. NW, Suite B
thepeoplescider.com

Thornapple Brewing Co.

6262 28th St., (616) 288-6907
thornapplebrewing.com

17

ENJOY FARM TO FORK DINING
AT TERRA

At Terra, in Eastown, local sourcing is more than a trendy fad, it's the philosophy of the business: to serve artisan, authentic, healthful food when it's in season. On a given day, the seared pork will have come from a Cassopolis farm; a house favorite, the red-skinned potatoes, from Zeeland; and other veggies, from Allendale.

1429 Lake Dr. SE, (616) 301-0998

SOME LIKE IT HOT
AT THE BELTLINE BAR

The Beltline Bar was so named because when it opened on the corner of 28th Street and Division Avenue, 28th Street was often called the Beltline. There have been several owners over the years, the most recent being Jeff Lobdell and his company, Restaurant Partners, Inc. It has grown from a forty-two-seat neighborhood bar to a large and favorite spot for Tex-Mex aficionados, and has received many awards, including "Best Margarita" and "Best Burrito" by *Grand Rapids Magazine*. It's no surprise the burrito came out on top, as it's a signature dish that came about during a moment of panic when the chef discovered (just before the lunch crowd was due!) that the supplier had mistakenly delivered the wrong size soft shells. He hastily came up with a new dish he called the Wet Burrito. It was an instant hit.

16 28th St. SE, Wyoming, (616) 245-0494
beltlinebar@4gr8food.com

19

DRINK CRAFT SPIRITS
AT LONG ROAD DISTILLERS

Visit Long Road Distillers, recently named the "Best Craft Specialty Spirits Distillery" in the country by the *USA Today*'s 10 Best Readers' Choice Travel Awards for the second year in a row. The distillery has gained national attention for their award-winning, locally sourced, and craft-distilled spirits. Whether your drink of choice is gin, vodka, brandy, whiskey, aquavit, or liqueur, Long Road has you covered.

Order small drinks so you can taste a variety of spirits and pick your favorites. They also serve tempting cocktails and food at the bar/restaurant.

Long Road conducts tours of their distillery on select dates, so check their schedule and make a reservation to learn about the craft of distilling spirits.

Long Road Distillers, 537 Leonard St. NW, (616) 228-4924
longroaddistillers.com

OTHER DISTILLERIES IN GRAND RAPIDS

Atwater Brewery

201 Michigan St. NW, (616) 649-3020
atwaterbeer.com

Bier Distillery

5295 West River Dr. NE, Ste. 100,
Comstock Park, (616) 888-9746
bierdistillery.com

Gray Skies Distillery

700 Ottawa NW, (616) 893-3305
grayskiesdistllery.com

Hemingway Lounge, Artesian Distillers

15 Ionia Ave. SW, (616) 446-6307
artesiandistillers.com

New Holland, The Knickerbocker

417 Bridge St. NW, (616) 345-5642
newhollandbrew.com/theknickerbocker

Thornapple Brewing Company

6262 28th St., (616) 288-6907
thornapplebrewing.com

FIND A FUTURE CELEBRITY CHEF
AT THE HERITAGE RESTAURANT

It could be said that Grand Rapids Community College is cooking up something new and wonderful. That can be taken literally when describing the Heritage Restaurant. The fine dining establishment is staffed by culinary students directly supervised by the chef and table service faculty of the Secchia Institute for Culinary Education. Students here earn an Associate Degree of Applied Arts and Sciences or a certificate in Culinary Arts in Restaurant Management, Baking and Pastry Arts, or Personal Chef. In 2016, GRCC opened the student-operated Fountain Hill Brewing Company and Peter's Pub, named for Peter Secchia, at the Fountain Street address. Some of the many hats that have been worn by Secchia are philanthropist, ambassador, and restaurateur. His Pietro's Italian Restaurant has long been a Grand Rapids favorite.

151 Fountain St. NE, (616) 234-3700
opentable.com/the-heritage-restaurant

21

VISIT SOVENGARD SCANDINAVIAN RESTAURANT

The Sovengard Scandinavian Restaurant and Biergarden, located in the busy Bridge Street corridor on the west side, serves food created from locally sourced ingredients. The menu changes seasonally, so you can experience a taste of Scandinavia with a Midwestern twist throughout the year.

443 Bridge St. NW, (616) 214-7207
sovengard.com

Landmark Blue Bridge by Grand Valley State University.
Photo credit: Christine Nyholm

MUSIC AND ENTERTAINMENT

22

ATTEND THE GRAND RAPIDS SYMPHONY

The Grand Rapids Symphony has brought pleasure to music lovers since 1930. Now offering ten concert series each year, the symphony definitely fulfills its mission "to share great music that moves the human soul." Selections are chosen for their ability to capture the imagination of young and old alike. Whatever your preference, you will find it among the Grand Rapids Pops, classical, chamber, holiday concerts, and more. Do yourself a favor and attend a concert outside your usual comfort zone. Chances are you'll be glad you did. Affiliated productions include the biennial Bach Festival, bringing the best of baroque to local audiences, Music for Health, Grand Rapids Symphony Youth Choruses, and numerous kid-friendly music concerts, starting with the Lollipop Concerts for the youngest of audiences. GRS also provides the orchestra for the Grand Rapids Ballet and Opera Grand Rapids.

Ticket office: 300 Ottawa Ave. NW, Ste. 100, (616) 454-9451
grsymphony.org

23

ENJOY BAR MUSIC

There are several spots that feature live music and amazing shows. The Intersection is one of the world's top mid-size concert venues and has hosted local and national music acts for more than forty years. The Orbit is a concert venue in the commercial district that presents a wide variety of musical acts in a venue equipped with five bar locations. There are also many bars and restaurants that offer live entertainment in the city.

The Intersection, 133 Grandville Ave. SW, (616) 451-8232
sectionlive.com

The Orbit Room, 2525 Eastbrook Blvd. SE, (616) 942-1328
orbitroom.com

SEE A SHOW
AT THE RENOWNED GRAND RAPIDS CIVIC THEATER

Theater buffs are lucky to have the Civic Theater, one of the largest of its kind in the United States. Since opening in 1925, the theater has grown, so each season is packed with offerings for every taste, be it musical, drama, comedy, or children's theater. Some shows are classics, while others are innovative. They're all professionally staged and sure to delight. If you're a ham at heart and would like to pursue acting, the GRCT School of Theater Arts is nationally recognized and has six-week classes for students ages four to adult. You can register for musical theater, acting, improv, and more. Along with the full format classes, shorter workshops are offered as well.

30 N. Division Ave., (616) 222-6650
grct.org

TIP

The GRCT is arguably the best, but it's by no means the only game in town. Also worthy of checking out:

Wealthy Street Theatre is an old movie house now showing movies and staging live performances.

Wealthy Street Theatre, 1130 Wealthy St. SE, (616) 459-4788
wealthytheatre.org

Circle Theater is a source of great entertainment offering five main shows and numerous concerts. Especially popular is the Magic Circle, retellings of old classics.

Circle Theater, 1703 Robinson Rd. SE, (616) 456-6656
circletheater.org

Other options include the Peter Martin Wege Theatre, Spectrum, Actors' Theatre, and Jewish Theatre.

The Dog Story Theater doesn't stage productions but offers a flexible and affordable venue for local talents to showcase their work.

LISTEN TO SOME OF THE BEST MUSIC IN TOWN

AT CALVIN COLLEGE

Most agree that the best of the best is the annual Handel's *Messiah* performed by the Calvin Oratio Society. The Society debuted with *Messiah* in 1920, and it remains a favorite and a staple on many local Christmas season must-do lists. Since then, the COS has steadily grown and offers a number of concerts each year with singers of all ages and all backgrounds, many of whom are professional musicians and/or music teachers. The Oratio Society is the best known, but Calvin offers a number of ensembles including campus, gospel, and alumni choirs; a jazz band; and an orchestra. All are worthy of your attention. Calvin College is operated by the Christian Reformed Church denomination, and its music department is internationally acclaimed.

1700 Fulton St. SE., (616) 632-2413
aquinas.edu/music/concerts-events

TIP

Aquinas College also has a great music department, with regularly scheduled programs.

26

ENJOY FREE SUMMER CONCERTS AT THE GRAM

Head downtown to the Grand Rapids Art Museum on summer Thursday evenings for a fun-filled, family-friendly variety of free concerts held outdoors on the GRAM terrace. Styles vary and are staged by regional musicians. Get up and boogie if you feel the urge. Make a night of it by having dinner at one of the many area eateries, or for a fun, casual experience, patronize the food trucks. Don't forget to sip your favorite beverage available at the cash bar. GRAM is open late on Thursdays so you can also get your art fix.

101 Monroe Center NW, (616) 831-2917
pr@artmuseum.org

GET OUT
AND DANCE

Get out and dance and enjoy the nightlife in Grand Rapids. Whether your taste in music runs to blues, rock, DJ, or electronic, there is a nightclub where you can dance to the beat.

Billy's Eastown, 1437 Wealthy St.
(616) 459-5757
billyslounge.com

Grand Woods Lounge, Downtown, 77 Grandville Ave.
(616) 451-4300
grandwoodslounge.com

The Pyramid Scheme, Heartside Neighborhood, 68 Commerce Ave. SW
(616) 272-3758
pyramidschemebar.com

Eve Nightclub at the B.O.B., Downtown, 20 Monroe Ave. NW
(616) 356-2000
thebob.com/evenightclub

TIP

GR Live on WYCE hosts a live radio show featuring the latest music news and top local artists. Stop in to see the show at the B.O.B. at noon on Thursdays or tune in to 88.1 FM.

WYCE.org or grcmc.org/wyce/GRLive

28

CATCH AN ART FILM
AT THE URBAN INSTITUTE OF CONTEMPORARY ART

One of the city's cultural gems is the 195-seat movie theater in the Urban Institute of Contemporary Art, West Michigan's largest center devoted to contemporary art. It is part of the Kendall College of Art and Design of Ferris State University. The theater is open year-round on Tuesdays through Sundays and offers a wide variety of films with something for every taste. One favorite is the annual series of Oscar-nominated short films.

Films range from independent, international, art, documentary, film festival award winners, and one-night screenings of classics. Also see everything from short films to home movies on Open Projector Nights.

TIP

While you're there check out the art exhibits and see if there are any classes you'd like to take.

2 Fulton St. W, (616) 454-7000
uica.org

BE ENCHANTED
BY BALLET

The Grand Rapids Ballet, Michigan's only professional ballet company, will celebrate its 50th anniversary in the 2021–22 season. The ballet is committed to lifting the human spirit through the art of dance. There are enchanting performances throughout the season, but a popular favorite is the classic Christmas ballet *The Nutcracker*, a magical favorite of children and adults alike.

341 Ellsworth SW, (616) 454-4771
grballet.com

ATTEND THE OPERA
AT THE BETTY VAN ANDEL OPERA CENTER

Opera in Grand Rapids once consisted only of touring companies passing through. By the mid-1900s, interest and public support grew to include small-scale operatic performances at the St. Cecilia Music Society. Then came the Opera Association of West Michigan and its first offering, a hugely successful performance of *The Marriage of Figaro*. That effort grew into today's vibrant Betty Van Andel Opera Center, which routinely stages such favorites as *La Traviata*, *La Boheme*, *Rigoletto*, *Carmen*, *The Magic Flute*, and more.

Education opportunities include the Betty Van Andel scholarship and the Children's Opera, which allows kids to perform and produce shows as part of the Creative Connections cultural education program. Master classes are also led by prominent opera scholars, performers, and directors. If you haven't yet attended an operatic performance, try it. Who knows? You may become a fan.

1320 E. Fulton St., (616) 451-2741
operagr.org

31

LISTEN TO THE MUSIC
OF THE BELLS

Grand Valley State University presents free Carillon Concerts at the Allendale campus and Grand Rapids campus during the summer months. Listen to the music of the ringing bells and enjoy the rich, inspirational sound for an uplifting experience.

The Cook Carillion's forty-eight bells at the Allendale campus were cast in the Netherlands in 1994. The Beckering Family Carillon's forty-eight bells in Grand Rapids were cast in France in 2000.

In a Carillion concert an expert carilloneur climbs the steps to the bell tower cabin and plays the bells. Video cameras transmit live images of the performance to a monitor at the base of the tower, so the audience can see how the music is played.

Allendale Campus, 1300 Thomas J. and Marcia J. Haas Center
for Performing Arts, Allendale, (616) 331-3484
gvsu.edu/music/carillon-at-gvsu-410.htm

Robert C. Pew Grand Rapids Campus, Lacks International Plaza at
Richard M. DeVos Center, 401 Fulton St. W, (616) 331-3484
gvsu.edu/music/carillon-at-gvsu-410.htm

The Grand Valley State University presents a variety of concerts, many of them free, throughout the year. Check the GVSU Department of Music, Theatre, and Dance Events Calendar for the list of scheduled performances.

gvsu.edu.mtd/module-events-view.htm

32

JAZZ AROUND

The West Michigan Jazz Society has a calendar of jazz events in venues around the city. The Society produces live music events and also supports the events hosted by other art organizations.

The Monday Night Jazz Series is held on the third Monday of each month from September through April (excluding December). The events are usually mainstream jazz but might also include other genres, such as Dixie and Latin. Locations for the jazz series rotate between venues, so check their website for information.

During the summer months they host Jazz in the Park, a series of ten live jazz concerts held at Ah-Nab-Awen Park. The events are on Monday nights from mid-June through mid-August.

wmichjazz.org

TIP

Grand Jazz Fest is a free two-day festival held at Rosa Parks Circle in August. The event brings notable artists and newcomers to the stage for a weekend of cool jazz.

grandjazzfest.org

SEE A SHOW
AT ANOTHER LOCAL FAVORITE VENUE, THE FOREST HILLS FINE ARTS CENTER

The Forest Hills community understood the value of such a facility and enthusiastically approved a bond referendum to finance the construction of a 62,000-square-foot facility with a 1,200-seat auditorium. There is an adjoining café for use during rehearsals and other events, as well as show intermissions. Fans love the annual subscription series of productions by traveling professional theatrical companies. The stage is also used for student performances by all schools in the district. The lobby has exhibit space for community artists, and an ever-changing roster of classes offers opportunities for all ages. When not otherwise in use, the space is used for conventions and other events.

600 Forest Hills Ave. SE, (616) 493-8965
fhfineartscenter.com

TIP

For an inexpensive theatrical experience, consider a high school production. The kids can use your support and you never know who you might see. Gillian Anderson began acting in junior high in Grand Rapids. In high school she produced and starred in a play. Who knows? You might snag some impressive "I knew her when" bragging rights.

CATCH A SHOW
AT THE SUBURBAN VAN SINGEL PERFORMING ARTS CENTER

For a theatrical experience to rival those put on downtown, look no further than Byron Center's Van Singel Performing Arts Center. Past favorite productions include *Hello Dolly*, *Fiddler on the Roof*, *The Sunshine Boys*, *The Seussical Musical*, and *A Christmas Carol*. The state-of-the-art facility within Byron Center High School was conceived in the mid-1990s with the announcement that a new high school would be built on 84th Street and Burlingame Avenue. A group of parents and local business leaders strongly believed exposure to, and experience in, the arts were valuable components in a well-rounded life. They proposed the theatre project to the Byron Center Public Schools Board of Education. The result is a completely self-supporting theater staging plays and concerts by touring productions, along with a showcase for regional talent.

8500 Burlingame Ave. SW, Byron Center, (616) 878-6800
vsfac.com

LISTEN TO MUSIC
AT THE NEW STUDIO C

Be among the first to experience the music at Studio C Listening Room, scheduled to open in September 2019. Studio C will be a key component of Studio Park, the exciting new entertainment complex south of Van Andel Arena.

The intimate 200-seat listening room will be a listening experience combined with a bar-restaurant feel, according to Quinn Matthews, who is stepping down as station manager of community radio station WYCE to direct and curate the listening room. Expect to see and hear national and local acts, jazz rock, bluegrass, folk music, comedy showcases, CD release shows, and everything in-between.

Studio Park, 123 Ionia Ave. SW

TIP

You can also experience live acoustic music at the pristine listening room at Seven Steps Up Live Music & Events Venue in Spring Lake. The 122-seat listening venue is in a historic Masonic Temple, which was originally built in 1919.

116 S. Jackson St., Spring Lake, (616) 678-3618
sevenstepsup.com

EXPERIENCE
BROADWAY THEATRE

Fifth Third Bank's Broadway Grand Rapids Series brings Broadway entertainment to Grand Rapids. Experience the best of Broadway at DeVos Performance Hall. Theater lovers in West Michigan experience the thrill of top-notch professional live entertainment and memorable music without traveling to New York. Check the schedule and get tickets to see great theater.

Broadway Grand Rapids presents top-flight shows like *School of Rock*, *The Book of Mormon*, *Waitress*, *On Your Feet!*, and *Anastasia*. Check the website for the current schedule of events.

122 Lyon St. NW, (616) 235-6285
broadwaygrandrapids.com

37

SOLVE A MYSTERY
OVER DINNER

Release your inner Agatha Christie and solve a mystery at a mystery dinner, where your dining companion might just be the guilty party.

The Dinner Detective interactive comedy murder mystery dinner show is performed at the Courtyard by Marriott in downtown Grand Rapids. The actors are not dressed in costume, so they blend in with guest sleuths in the audience. Guests analyze clues to find the prime suspect and ultimately the murderer.

Another mystery dinner show is the Mystery Dinner Party, where guests get to experience an evening of intrigue and fun. The murderer will be sitting right at one of the tables while guests sort out clues over a three-course dinner. Murder mystery dinner shows are held at Pietro's Italian Restaurant.

The Dinner Detective, (866) 496-0535
thedinnerdetective.com/grand-rapids

Murder Mystery Dinner, (888) 643-2583
grimprov.com

TIP

The Dinner Detective and the Murder Mystery Company also serve up mystery shows for private events, so this would be fun for a group or organization.

LAUGH FOR THE HEALTH OF IT
AT GILDA'S LAUGHFEST

Gilda's LaughFest, the first-ever community-wide festival of laughter in the nation, is a major ten-day Midwest festival based in Grand Rapids in March. The multi-venue celebration of laughter includes comedic events throughout West Michigan. The festival was created by Gilda's Club Grand Rapids and celebrates "laughter for the health of it." LaughFest attracts an average of 50,000 attendees to West Michigan, so join in the fun and get ready to laugh.

LaughFest events have been held at DeVos Performance Hall, DeVos Place, Gun Lake Casino, Larkin's The Other Place, Pyramid Scheme, Dr. Grins, Vander Mill, and the Wealthy Theatre. There are categories of shows, including 21+ for adults, clean comedy, improv and sketch, music and theatre, stand-up, and other seriously funny stuff.

Passes can be purchased at the LaughFest website, laughfestgr.org

TIP

Gilda Radner was a Detroit native who found fame on *Saturday Night Live*, with hilarious characters like Rosanne Rosannadanna and Lisa Loopner and Emily Litella ("Never mind!"). The gifted comedian died of ovarian cancer in 1989 and Gilda's Club was started by her husband, Gene Wilder, and therapist Joanna Bull to support people afflicted by cancer, with cancer support, grief support, and education. Gilda's LaughFest benefits the mission of Gilda's Club Grand Rapids, so you can support a great cause while laughing.

1806 Bridge St. NW, (616) 453-8300
gildasclubgr.org

Ice skating at Rosa Parks Circle.
Photo credit: Christine Nyholm

SPORTS AND RECREATION

39

ROOT, ROOT, ROOT
FOR THE WEST MICHIGAN WHITECAPS

The West Michigan Whitecaps Class A minor league baseball team plays home games at the Fifth Third Ballpark in Comstock Park. Affiliated with the Detroit Tigers, the team boasts not one, but three mascots: Crash, the River Rascal; Roxy, the River Rascal; and Franky, the Swimming Pig. Among the many players who have gone on to major league teams are Casey Crosby, Matt Joyce, Nicholas Castellano, and Ramon Santiago. Prior to joining the Tigers, the team played for the Oakland Athletics. The Whitecaps won divisional and regional titles in 1996, 1998, 2004, 2006, 2007, and 2015.

4500 West River Dr., Comstock Park
whitecaps-baseball.com

SUPPORT
THE DRIVE

Of course, a sports-loving town like Grand Rapids will also have a semi-pro basketball team. Since 2014, the Grand Rapids Drive has satisfied that need. The Detroit Pistons affiliate began life as the Anaheim Arsenal, an expansion team in the NBA Anaheim Arsenal Development League. They left Anaheim with the worst record in the league. From there they played in Springfield, Massachusetts, as the Springfield Armor, where they did a little better. They have not yet won a championship, but are looking better since coming to Michigan, where they made it to the playoffs for the second time in 2017–18. They lost to the Raptors in the first round. The team's office is downtown, but they play at the Deltaplex at 2500 Turner Ave. NW.

40 Monroe Circle NW, Ste. 2000, 844-GRDRIVE

ICE SKATE
AT ROSA PARKS CIRCLE

One of the city's best places to ice skate is at Rosa Parks Circle, centrally located downtown. The season lasts three months, from mid-November through mid-February. Skates are available for rental, as are balance aids for those new to the sport or whose skills have gotten rusty. Lockers and shoe bins can also be rented. The rink is operated by the city of Grand Rapids. There is a small admission charge. When you are done skating, warm up with coffee or steaming hot chocolate at one of the many Monroe Center options.

135 Monroe Center NW, (616) 456-3699
grandrapidsmi.gov/government/departments/parks-and-recreation

DOWNHILL SKI
AT CANNONSBURG

Whether beginner or pro, downhill skiers can find their winter outdoor bliss at the Cannonsburg Ski Area. With twenty-one runs, it's easy to find a perfect fit for any level of experience. One run is 1,500 feet long with a vertical drop of 250 feet, the highest in southwest Michigan. The resort offers lessons, equipment rentals, and a fully stocked ski shop. Activity options range from Mountain Minnies, a program designed for fun in the snow for two- to five-year-old-girls, all the way up to an adult race league. Tubing is also an option, along with trails for cross-country skiing or mountain biking. Take a break in the snack shop or lunch in one of the two cafeterias.

6800 Cannonsburg Rd., Belmont, (616) 874-6711
cannonsburg.com

43

CHEER ON
THE GRAND RAPIDS GRIFFINS

Hockey fans can catch Griffins home games downtown at the Van Andel Arena. Grand Rapids had not had a pro hockey team since the 1970s when Dave Van Andel and Dan DeVos formed West Michigan Hockey, Inc. in 1995 to buy a NHL minor league franchise. To make sure that would happen, they first built the Van Andel Arena. The Griffins brought home two AHL Conference championships, five AHL Division championships, and two Calder Cups. Since 2002, they have been affiliated with the Detroit Red Wings. Ninety-seven former Griffins have since played in the major league, including fifteen who were on the Detroit Red Wings playoff roster in 2008 when Detroit won the coveted Stanley Cup.

Van Andel Arena, 130 W. Fulton St., (616) 742-6600
vanandelarena.com

44

RUN A MARATHON

The Grand Rapids Marathon has been going strong since 2004. Participants consider it fun because it feels more personal than the circus-like atmosphere of the larger ones, like the Boston Marathon. Organizers say the race supports every runner and celebrates individual accomplishments in a spirit of friendship and community. Winning is a good thing, but it's not the only thing. There is also a half-marathon for those not quite ready for the bigtime.

grandrapidsmarathon.com

TIP

Most people who run will never do a marathon. For them there are numerous other races to run and are often part of a larger festival or event. For more information, check the events calendar in local publications, look online, or contact Experience Grand Rapids.

45

GO CROSS-COUNTRY SKIING

AND GLIDE ACROSS THE SNOW

Experience the exhilaration of cross-country skiing on the scenic trails of the Kent County Parks. The Park District grooms the trails at Palmer Park, which is one of the most popular cross-country ski destinations in town. There are three groomed trails, each of which is two miles long, for a total of six miles of trails. Meander through the woods, along the streams, and across the open fairways at the golf course. The trailheads are at the Kaufman Golf Course clubhouse, which can be accessed from Clyde Park Avenue. There is a trail fee of $2 per person or $25 for a season pass. Ski rentals are available at the clubhouse.

Robinette's has walking and cross-country skiing trails that you can use for free. Trail maps are available in the bakery, so pick up a map and take to the trails for fun and brisk exercise.

Palmer Park, 1275 52nd St. SW, Wyoming
kentcountyparks.org/trails/crossountryskitrails

Robinette's Apple Haus & Winery, 3142 4 Mile Rd. NE, (616) 361-5567
robinettes.com

The park district also offers ungroomed cross-country ski trails at its other area parks, including Seidman Park, Pickerel Lake Park, Millennium Park, Donald J. Lamoreaux Park, Leopard Preserve, Luton Park, Provin Trails Park, Rogue River Park, Townsend Park, and Wahlfield Park.

46

GET A SQUIRREL'S EYE VIEW AT TREERUNNER ADVENTURE PARK

If you're not afraid of heights and enjoy adventure, head to the TreeRunner Park. Opened by a team of Michigan entrepreneurs in 2015, there are now two parks in Michigan and a third in North Carolina. Aerial adventure courses like the TreeRunner are a new trend and comprise obstacle courses with varying degrees of difficulty. Think military training or Outward Bound. These take place in trees and include zip lines, ropes courses, barrels, nets, and bridges that are connected between platforms built around trees. Safety comes first, and the park is held to the standards set by the Association for Challenge Course Technology and includes a belay system to maximize safety. There are courses for all levels of ability, including a new Junior Park for children as young as four.

2121 Celebration Dr. NE, (616) 226-3993
grandrapids@treerunnerparks.com

TAKE A HIKE

AT AMAN PARK AND TAKE TIME TO SMELL THE WILDFLOWERS

If it's true that walking is the best form of exercise, then there's no better place to indulge than the trails at Aman Park in between Rapids and Standale on Lake Michigan Drive between 14th Avenue and Trillium Drive. It's heavily wooded with Sand Creek running through it. Two bridges are strategically placed for crossing the crystal-clear creek. It's open all year so cross-country skiers can also enjoy the trails. A map shows how trails intersect so you can customize your adventure, thus avoiding hills if you're a bit out of shape. Enjoy the natural beauty during any season, but during the spring you'll find it blanketed with colorful wildflowers including bellwort, buttercups, Virginia bluebells, Dutchman's breeches, trillium, wild geranium, and jack-in-the-pulpit. Overhead, flowering dogwoods bloom.

1859 Lake Michigan Dr., Standale

BE A RIVER RAT

When you're lucky enough to be in a river town, make use of the river. Kayak, raft, or canoe on the Grand. Go fishing. Picnic on its banks. Photograph it from the blue bridge downtown. Best of all, this costs nothing if you do it on your own. If you're in the mood for something more, cruise the river on the paddleboat *The Grand Lady*. History buffs will see the river as the pioneers did when that was the only mode of transportation available.

825 Taylor St., Jenison, (616) 457-4837
rivercruises@grandlady.info

WATCH
THE HOTTEST SPORTS COMPETITION IN TOWN

2019 will be the 98th year Calvin College of Grand Rapids and Hope College in nearby Holland have been basketball rivals. The Division III schools play each other two or three times a year and is probably the most closely matched rivalry in college basketball. Both are Christian schools; Calvin is Christian Reformed, and Hope is affiliated with the Reformed Church in America. Once one denomination, they broke apart in 1857. When the teams have met in playoff games at the Van Andel Arena in Grand Rapids, the arena filled to its capacity of nearly 12,000. It is a rivalry closely watched, not only in West Michigan, but nationally. At the end of 2018, Hope held a narrow edge of five games.

50

PLAY A ROUND
OF GOLF

The city-owned Indian Trails Golf Course was renovated in 2017 and, after 90 years, still remains a local favorite. Kent County owns the Kaufman Golf Course in Wyoming, which is thought to be a bit more challenging and is the home of the Kent County Amateur Golf Tournament. Local history buffs will remember that the Kaufman course is built over the old Picric Acid Plant, a munitions plant started, but never completed, after WWI. Be sure to also try the family-owned Maple Hill course. Even if you play elsewhere, Maple Hill is the best place around to shop for clubs, balls, clothing, and everything else that is golf-related.

Indian Trails Golf Course, 2776 Kalamazoo Ave. SE
(616) 245-2026
indiantrailsgc.org

Kaufman Golf Course, 4807 Clyde Park Ave. SW, Wyoming
(616) 538-5050
kentcountyparks.org/kaufman

Maple Hill Golf Course, 5510 Invanrest Ave. SW, Wyoming
(616) 538-0290
maplehillgolf.com

TIP
You can also go fat tire biking
at Indian Trails.

51

GO SWIMMING
AT THE BEACH

Spending the day at the beach is one of the classic pleasures of summer, so grab a swimsuit, slather on the sunscreen, and head to the beach to swim in the water and play in the sand.

Western Michigan is home to some of the best beaches in America, just 30 minutes west of Grand Rapids. You can take a day trip to enjoy the sugar sand beaches of Lake Michigan and stay to watch the spectacular sunset over the lake. Take a romantic walk in the sand, build sand castles, jump in the waves, cool off in the water, or just bask in the sun . . . it's a day at the beach.

If you want to stay in the city, you can still enjoy a day at the beach at Millennium Park, which is one of four beaches in the Kent County Park system. The beaches at Long Lake Park in Sparta, Myers Lake Park in Rockford, and Wabasis Lake Park in Greenville are free to use. There is a daily use fee to use the beach at Millennium Park, unless visitors purchase a season pass.

Millennium Park, 1415 Maynard Ave. SW, Walker
kentcountyparks.org/millennium

Long Lake Park, 13747 Krauskopf Rd. NE, Sparta
kentcountyparks.org/longlake

Myers Lake Park, 7350 Hessler Dr., Rockford
kentcountyparks.org/myerslake

Wabasis Lake Park, 11220 Springhill Dr., Greenville
kentcountyparks.org/wabisislakepark

TIP

Drive west for a day at the beaches of Lake Michigan. You can find beaches in Grand Haven, Holland, Muskegon, Ferryburg, Spring Lake, and Saugatuck. Beaches that are in the State Park system will require Michigan Resident Recreation Passport or will charge a use fee. There is a listing of beaches on the Experience Grand Rapids website.

experiencegrandrapids.com/things-to-do/beaches

GO THREE-ON-THREE
WITH GUS

The Gus Macker Three-on-Three Basketball Tournament, now a national event, began with eighteen players in the McNeal family's driveway. Each threw in a dollar for a winner-take-all purse. Brothers Scott and Mitch McNeal organized the event in 1974. Scott's childhood nickname was Gus Macker, and he was a short kid who wanted to play basketball. Over the years it evolved into more than 1,500 sanctioned tournaments involving 2.7 million players and 27.5 million spectators watching the double-elimination event. A consolation bracket, affectionately known as the Toilet Bowl, comprises teams that lose their first two games. A computer picks the men's and women's teams, factoring in age, height, and experience. They are bracketed into three categories: Junior, Adult, and Top. All games are refereed by registered officials. "Family fun in a festival atmosphere" is how the tournament sees itself, with games played in various downtown streets, parking lots, and neighborhood parks. Another important part of the mix is that a percentage of the proceeds from each tournament go to one or more charitable organizations in the community where it takes place. Nonprofit organizations raise additional funds by operating on-site concessions. Since 1987, Macker tournaments have raised $16 million for worthwhile local charities. And it all started because one kid wanted to play basketball!

103 E. Main St., Belding, (616) 794-1445
macker.com

53

JOIN A POOL LEAGUE

The American Pool Players Association has a local franchise, APA of West Michigan, operated by Jenison resident Rhonda Ayers. According to Ayers, there are two types of players, the rabid and those who just enjoy the social aspects of the game. Her league is for the latter, people who just want to go out and play pool while enjoying a beer or two. If that sounds like you, join the fun. It must be fun because she started with twenty teams and now has 220. You will play weekly and have opportunities to play in a variety of tournaments, some of which you have to qualify for, and qualifications vary with each. The ones that are the most fun are open to all league players and are played for a cause. An annual favorite benefits Toys for Tots. Ayers has run tournaments to raise money for breast cancer, other health issues, and for league members who have fallen on hard times. She even organized one to buy a headstone for a player who died unexpectedly at age forty. There is also a Junior League for children ages seven to eighteen.

Rhonda Ayers, (616) 292-8599
westmichigan.apaleagues.com

54

TRY BOWLING A PERFECT 300

While there's nothing new or trendy about bowling, it remains a popular activity for one reason: It's fun! Whether league play, family fun, or a children's birthday party, everyone enjoys rolling a strike or feels the same frustration in trying to pick up that pesky 7–10 split. Gutter ball? No problem; it happens to the best of us. One of the best spots to bowl in Grand Rapids has long been AMF Eastbrook Lanes. These lanes have remained relevant by adapting to our changing times with the addition of other elements to entice an already loyal clientele. Along with bowling a few frames on one of the forty lanes, you can shoot pool, play the arcade games, and top it all off with pizza or other food choices in the sports bar.

3500 Lake Eastbrook Blvd. SE, (616) 949-7650
amf.com/location/amf-eastbrooklanes

55

RIDE YOUR MOUNTAIN BIKE

There might not be mountains here, but there are an abundance of mountain bike trails, some within a twenty-minute drive of downtown. *Outside* magazine in 2010 named Grand Rapids the best town for mountain biking. There are trails for every skill level, shown on maps in green for easy, blue for intermediate, and black for advanced.

The best of the best:

Merrell Trail, 8320 Belmont Rd., Rockford
Recommended for advanced

Luton Park Trail, 5950 10 Mile Rd., Rockford
Recommended for beginners

Egypt Valley Trail, 6800-6820 4 Mile Rd., Ada

Cannonsburg Ski Area, 6800 Cannonsburg Rd., Belmont

Wahlfield Park, 6811 Alpine Ave., Comstock Park

Yankee Springs Recreation Area, 2526 S. Yankee Springs Rd., Middleville

For more information, contact Experience Grand Rapids, experiencegr.com

DON'T OVERLOOK
THE YMCA

It may seem like a no-brainer, but if it's been awhile since you visited a Y, check one out. You'll be amazed at the options offered. Just west of downtown, on Lake Michigan Drive, is the David D. Hunting YMCA, the first LEED-certified (Leadership in Energy and Environmental Design) Y in the country. Named for one of the Steelcase Corporation founders, its possibilities are unlimited. And all at reasonable cost. What do *you* need? Childcare, swimming (four pools!), exercise equipment, strength training, a climbing wall, running track, kid zone, teen zone, kid and teen activities, arts and humanities, an ever-changing roster of health and fitness classes, sports leagues, personal training, sauna, whirlpool . . . the list goes on. And on. There's even a chapel.

475 Lake Michigan Dr. NW, (616) 855-9622
grymca.org/david-d-hunting

OTHER YMCAs IN THE GREATER GRAND RAPIDS AREA

Mary Free Bed YMCA

5500 Burton St. SE

Spartan Stores YMCA

5722 Metro Way SW, Wyoming

Visser Family YMCA

3540 Fairlanes Ave. SW, Grandville

JINGLE THOSE BELLS
WITH A WINTER SLEIGH RIDE

Bundle up against the winter cold and experience the old-fashioned pleasure of gliding across the snow in a sleigh drawn by horses. Horse-drawn sleigh rides are a fun activity for the family or a great romantic date. The sleigh travels through the farm fields and wooded areas, letting you enjoy the beauty of the countryside with loved ones and friends.

When there is no snow, you can go on a horse-drawn hayride for a nostalgic ride through the countryside.

Fruit Ridge Hayrides, 11966 Fruit Ridge NW, Kent City
(616) 887-5052
fruitridgehayrides.com

Post Family Farm, 5081 Bauer Rd., Hudsonville
(616) 669-1964
postfamilyfarm.com

Teusink's Pony Farm Sleigh Rides, 1468 West 32nd St., Holland
(616) 335-6226
teusinksponyfarm.com

EXPLORE THE NATURAL WETLANDS
AT MILLENNIUM PARK

Millennium Park offers an extensive network of trails on 1,400 acres where you can experience nature. There are several large lakes and wetland areas where you can observe wildlife, relax, hike, and learn about nature. Start with the Hansen Nature Trail at the corner of Butterworth and Riverbend Drives for an easy loop for hiking with scenic views of the lake and nearby wetlands.

Millennium Park, 1415 Maynard Ave. SW, Walker
kentcountyparks.org/millennium/activities

TIP

The entire family will have fun playing in the snow and exercising with snow sports at Millennium Park during the snowy winter months. While the main recreation area of the park is closed in the winter, the trails are busy with cross-country skiers, snow-runners, and people on snowshoes.

The off-season parking lot is available on the east side of Maynard Ave. and at the trailhead at Butterworth and O'Brien.

Grand Rapids Public Museum Carousel.
Photo credit: Grand Rapids Public Museum

CULTURE AND HISTORY

VISIT
A GIGANTIC HORSE

A horse is a horse, of course, of course, unless that horse is cast in bronze, is twenty-four feet tall, and weighs fifteen tons. Then it's *The American Horse*, the crown jewel of the Frederik Meijer Gardens and Sculpture Park.

Its story began in the 1490s when Lodovico Sforza commissioned Leonardo Da Vinci to sculpt the world's largest horse. Leonardo drew sketches, created a model, and acquired metal for what he believed would be his greatest work. Then France invaded Italy and his metal became ammunition. He died still mourning his lost masterpiece.

A 1977 *National Geographic* article led to a failed attempt to create Leonardo's horse that never was. Then Fred Meijer, philanthropist and one-stop-shopping pioneer, took over. He hired Japanese American sculptor Nina Akamu, who, using the few extant Da Vinci sketches, created the horse as it stands today. Two horses were cast, then the mold was destroyed.

Il Cavallo was unveiled in Milan, Italy, on September 19, 1999, five hundred years to the day after the French invasion. *The American Horse* was unveiled a month later in Grand Rapids.

More than a one-horse attraction, the sculpture park is home to more than fifty major works and is internationally acclaimed. The gardens, too, are not to be missed.

Other special exhibits and happenings that make this a worthwhile destination include:

- A spring butterfly habitat
- Outdoor concerts in the summer months
- A "Christmas around the world" exhibit
- Year-round children's activities

1000 E. Beltline Ave. NE, (616) 957-1580
meijergardens.org

60

PAY YOUR RESPECTS
TO A FORMER PRESIDENT

Stop by the Gerald R. Ford Presidential Museum and learn about the 38th president. Not many cities can lay claim to a president, but we in Grand Rapids can. Gerald R. Ford ascended to the White House in 1974, after the resignation of President Nixon. Ford, though born in Nebraska, grew up in Grand Rapids, where he was a star football player at South High School. He married Elizabeth "Betty" Boomer in 1948, and the couple made their home in East Grand Rapids. He represented Michigan's Fifth Congressional District for twelve consecutive terms and rose to the position of House Minority Leader. Ford became vice president in 1973 following the resignation of Spiro Agnew and a year later became president when Richard Nixon also resigned.

Ford's museum is in Grand Rapids, his presidential library is in Ann Arbor, at his alma mater, the University of Michigan, where he also played football. He described the museum as "not a monument to any one man or any one presidency. Rather, it is a classroom of American democracy where school kids as well as scholars will enjoy access to the innermost workings of their government."

At the Ford Museum you will see a replica of the Oval Office and displays about the White House years, Ford family life, the bicentennial, the energy crisis, Queen Elizabeth II's visit, and more.

303 Pearl St. NW, (616) 254-0400
fordlibrarymuseum.gov

STEP BACK INTO THE PAST
AT THE PUBLIC MUSEUM

There's always something new and exciting here. The most popular permanent collection tells the story of the city's long-time reign as Furniture City, with examples of furniture made by the giants of the time: Phoenix, Stickley, Berkey and Gay, Imperial, Widdicomb, Sligh, Hekman, and others. You can also browse eleven Gaslight Village shops recreated from the 1890s (3/4 scale) and see how people shopped before malls. Another exhibit introduces you to the Natives who first lived on the Grand River. Enjoy the music of the Mighty Wurlitzer Pipe Organ, built in 1928. If it seems familiar, it's because it first entertained patrons of the Roaring Twenties Pizza Parlor who enjoyed the pizza and fun singalongs. Have lunch at the museum café overlooking the river. End your visit by mounting a bejeweled horse, a giraffe, tiger, goat, camel, whale, deer, or simply take a seat on one of the two chariots for a ride on the beautiful antique Spillman carousel. It's a must if you're there with children, and fun even if you're not.

272 Pearl St. NW, (616) 929-1700
grpm.org

VISIT THE ROGER B. CHAFFEE PLANETARIUM

Also part of the Grand Rapids Public Museum is the Roger B. Chaffee Planetarium. Chaffee's parents were living in suburban Wyoming when he was named to the space program, and were still there when Chaffee, Virgil "Gus" Grissom, and Edward White lost their lives in a launch pad fire in the Apollo 1 spacecraft in 1967. Grand Rapids remembers its fallen hero with the Planetarium, a street named for him in suburban Kentwood, and a statue downtown. Shows vary and include the new *Queen Light Show*, *The Little Star That Could*, and *Under Starlit Skies*, among others.

272 Pearl St. NW, (616) 929-1700
grpm.org

TIP

For another out-of-this-world experience, visit the James C. Veen Observatory in Lowell. It is owned and operated by the Grand Rapids Amateur Astronomical Association and is open to the public on the 2nd and 4th Saturdays from April through October. The observatory has telescopes, but visitors are welcome to bring their own. Note: it's only open if skies are clear. If in doubt, call to confirm.

3308 Kissing Rock Ave. SE, (616) 897-7065
graac.org

63

ESCAPE TO THE BLANDFORD NATURE CENTER

The Blandford Nature Center is another local gem with year-round things to do. All revolve around the center's mission to invite the community to enjoy, explore, and learn in nature. This is accomplished in a number of ways, from hiking eleven trails with varying degrees of difficulty, cross-country skiing, a farm with playful goats and organic produce, educational programs on topics including pioneer life and animal habitats, and days camps for kids during the summer, to name but a few. A seasonal favorite is maple sugaring when the sap runs in spring. It's impossible to talk about the nature center without mentioning its first and longest-serving director, Mary Jane Dockery, who was the heart of the organization and could be seen there volunteering long after her retirement. When Victor Blandford donated the land, Mary Jane's passion made it a continually evolving reality.

1715 Hillburn Ave. NW, (616) 735-6240
blandfordnaturecenter.org

MUG WITH THE MONKEYS
AT JOHN BALL PARK AND ZOO

The zoo's management works to ensure the animals are kept in as natural a habitat as possible. They are continually adding to the attractions, and not just with new animals, though each spring's crop of babies is worth a trip. A top zoo priority has always been education. This is accomplished through ongoing programs on animal habitat, Michigan wildlife, and wildlife conservation, among many more. School tours are planned with Common Core elements in mind. The zoo offers summer camp opportunities and sleepovers for kids in its own Zoo School. Among the animals exhibited, you'll find Van Andel Living Shores Aquarium, which includes penguins, Pelican Pier, Treasures of the Tropics, African Primates, and much more. Along the Idema Forest Realm are play zones for children, the Treetops Outpost, and overlooks from which to watch the wolves and polar bears. Don't forget the Petting Corral and the Funicular.

1300 W. Fulton St., (616) 336-4300
jbzoo.org

65

EXPLORE
THE GRAND RAPIDS ART MUSEUM

Visit the Grand Rapids Art Museum, which has more than 6,000 works of art, including American, European American, and European nineteenth- and twentieth-century paintings and sculpture. Guests are welcome to explore the collection. The museum is internationally known for its design and LEED Gold-certified status. Check their schedule for traveling exhibitions, special programs, workshops in the GRAM Studio, gallery tours, artist talks, live concerts, and more.

101 Monroe Center St. NW, (616) 831-1000
artmuseumgr.org

TIP

Admission to GRAM is free on Meijer Free Days, thanks to a generous gift from Meijer. The free admission is currently on Tuesdays from 10 a.m. to 5 p.m. and Thursday nights from 5 p.m. to 9 p.m. Please check the website to verify the days and times of free admission.

66

TOUR FRANK LLOYD WRIGHT'S
MEYER MAY HOUSE

Experience the stunning Prairie style architecture of Frank Lloyd Wright at the historic Meyer May House, which has been meticulously restored by the Grand Rapids–based Steelcase Corporation. Meyer May House affords visitors a glimpse of the genius of the famed architect.

The Meyer May House was completed in 1909 and stood out for its revolutionary contemporary design amid the ornate Victorian houses of the Heritage Hill area. This was Wright's first major commission in the state of Michigan.

Steelcase purchased the Meyer May House in 1985 and began an extensive two-year restoration. They rebuilt the roof to restore the dramatic cantilevered design, replaced plaster ceilings, restored a Niedecken mural, and repaired and cleaned more than one hundred beautiful art glass windows and skylights. The interior was furnished with original pieces and reproductions to recreate the space as it was in 1909.

The historic landmark was opened to the public in 1987. Visitors are able to appreciate the house as it was originally envisioned by Wright. Tours are free and take about ninety minutes, so plan to arrive early enough to take the time to enjoy the experience. Free tours are currently available on Tuesdays and Thursdays from 10 a.m. to 1 p.m. and Sundays from 1 to 4 p.m. You can also view an online tour on the website.

450 Madison Ave. SE, (616) 246-4821
meyermayhouse.steelcase.com

TIP

Meyer May House is located in the historic Heritage Hill neighborhood, so when you visit take the time to walk or drive around to see the fascinating historic architecture in the area.

EXPERIENCE
OUTDOOR ART

Grand Rapids has an abundance of outdoor art. One exciting project is the Grand Rapids Community Legends Project, sponsored by the Peter Secchia Family Foundation. One statue will be unveiled every two years until twenty-five legendary residents have been honored. Already in place are Lucius Lyon, one of the city's founders; Bishop Fredric Baraga, the famed missionary "snowshoe priest"; Chief Noonday, an early Ottawa leader; Jay Van Andel, business leader and philanthropist; Lyman S. Parks, Sr., the city's first black mayor; Stanley Ketchel, middleweight boxing champion; Betty Ford, First Lady and founder of the Betty Ford Clinic; Anna Sutherland Bissell, who ran a large corporation after the death of her husband; Helen Claytor, who was the first black president of the national YWCA; and William Alden Smith, United States congressional representative and senator who led the investigation of the sinking of the *Titanic* and whose extensive research was used in making the movie.

While strolling around the city, you will also happen upon *La Grande Vitesse*, the Fish Ladder, statues of Gerald R. Ford, Arthur Vandenberg, Roger B. Chaffee, and more. Two of the more popular murals appear downtown at the Children's Museum and on the Northwest corner of Division Avenue and Cherry Street. The latter depicts the city's Furniture City glory days. Pick up the Experience Grand Rapids walking tour map of downtown murals and sculptures.

68

GET YOUR FESTIVAL FIX

Summer is festival season. In Grand Rapids the biggest and best is the annual Festival of the Arts held on the first weekend in June. In 2019, the city will celebrate the festival's 50th anniversary. It all began with LaGrande Vitesse, the forty-three-foot-tall Alexander Calder stabile downtown. The Calder was cause to celebrate, so the first festival occurred downtown at Calder Square. It has since grown exponentially and honors all art forms: dance, music, literature and media, visual arts, performing arts, and design. Artists showcased represent the counties of Kent, Ottawa, Ionia, Allegan, Muskegon, Montcalm, Barry, and Newaygo. No longer just in Calder Square, it has spread all over the downtown area. Come for the live performances on multiple stages. Come for the camaraderie. Come for the food. Best of all, performances, displays, and all children's activities are free. Bring the whole family. There's something here for everyone!

festivalgr.org

TIP

Grand Rapids has other festivals, including Celebration on the Grand and as many ethnic festivals as there are immigrant groups. Suburbanites also find something to celebrate.

FIND A FESTIVAL

Join in the fun at the festivals around Grand Rapids celebrating art, music, dance, food, drink, ethnic cultures, and special interests. People love to be social, surrounding themselves with gaiety and lively activities at the large, festive gatherings. Look up information on the individual websites or check the listing of events at ExperienceGR.com/Events.

Irish on Ionia is Michigan's largest St. Patrick's Day Street Party.
irishonionia.com

Meijer LPGA Classic for Simply Give at Blythefield Country Club
meijerlpgaclassic.com

Grand Rapids Asian Pacific Festival at Rosa Parks Circle, grasianfestival.com

Grand Rapids Pride Festival, GRPride.org/festival

Grand Rapids Yassou! Greek Cultural Festival at Holy Trinity Greek Orthodox Church, grgreekfest.com

Grand JazzFest at Rosa Parks Circle, grandjazzfest.org

Hispanic Festival of Grand Rapids at Calder Plaza
hispanic-center.org/event/hispanic

Mexican Heritage Association Fiesta Mexicana

African American Arts & Music Festival at Calder Plaza

Oktoberfest West Michigan hosted by Edelweiss Club of Grand Rapids at John Ball Park, oktoberfestgr.com

International Wine, Beer & Food Festival at DeVos Place
grwinefestival.com

70

TOUR HISTORIC MANSIONS

See how the movers and shakers of the city's early days lived. Thirteen hundred historic houses were built in the nineteenth and early twentieth centuries by furniture and lumber barons, retail giants, manufacturing heavyweights, and professionals. The area boasts sixty types of architecture, including Italianate, Queen Anne, Greek Revival, and Prairie, and was almost lost in the 1960s, a decade of numerous urban renewal projects. One such proposal would have meant razing about 75 percent of the neighborhood. A cadre of residents, spearheaded by Barbara Roelofs, formed the Heritage Hill Neighborhood Association and proved you *can* fight city hall. It was too late to save everything, including the home built by Melville and Anna Bissell, who manufactured Bissell carpet sweepers, but the association's success became a model for communities nationwide in their fights to save historic treasures. Since 1968, residents have opened their homes for the Annual Heritage Hill House Tour, always held on the first weekend in May.

126 College Ave. SE, (616) 459-8950
heritage@heritagehillweb.org

GATHER WITH NATIVE AMERICANS AT A POW WOW

Native American tribes honor the tradition of their forefathers with an annual Pow Wow at Riverside Park. The Grand Valley American Indian Lodge Pow Wow is a colorful annual event that features Indian dances in native dress and fancy costumes, music, food, and crafts. All Indian organizations, tribal groups, and the general public are welcome. The foundation is a volunteer-operated non-profit dedicated to the preservation of Native American culture. Listen to the beat of the drums and watch the dancers as you learn about the customs and traditions of the Native American tribes. The Pow Wow is an alcohol-free, drug-free event and is family friendly. Check the Gathering Thunder website for information about the Pow Wow, which is held in September.

Riverside Park, Monroe Ave.
gatheringthunderfoundation.org
grps.org/NAEP

TIP

The Grand Valley State University's Celebrating All Walks of Life Pow Wow is held in the spring at the GVSU Fieldhouse Arena at the Allendale campus.

gvsu.edu.oma

72

ROLL OUT THE BARREL

AND HAVE A BARREL OF FUN DURING PULASKI DAYS

Everyone is Polish for one autumn week when the city celebrates Pulaski Days. In 1973 Ed Czyzyk and Walter Ulanch decided the Polish of the area should share their heritage with the community at large, and also honor General Casmir Pulaski. The Polish immigrant was a Revolutionary War hero who had been born into European nobility and gave his life defending freedom in his adopted country. One day soon turned into a weekend, and over the years, evolved into a whole week. Festivities take place in fourteen venues around the city, including the 5th Street, Diamond Street, St. Ladislaw, and Kosciuszki halls. Events include a kielbasa-eating contest, parade, and Polish Catholic mass. Flags are raised, a queen is crowned, and raffles won. All are welcome to polka, eat, and raise a glass.

Mailing address: P.O. Box 22371, Grand Rapids, MI 49501
pulaskidays.org

73

WATCH SALMON
SWIM UPSTREAM

Can something be a work of art and at the same time help migratory fish navigate the Grand River? It can if it is the Fish Ladder, installed in 1974 and designed by local sculptor Joseph Kinnebrew. The ladder is a series of pools arranged like stairs that allow fish, including salmon, trout, and steelhead, to bypass the sometimes raging water at the Sixth Street dam as they swim to their spawning grounds. It is fun to cheer them on as they leap from one pool to the next. Even when the fish aren't running, Fish Ladder Park is a calm oasis amid the bustle of the city, and the ladder itself is worthy of checking out and photographing. To see the ladder in use, plan your visit in spring or late summer.

560 Front St. NW, (616) 456-3696
michigan.org/property/fish-ladder-park

TAKE YOUR INNER GEARHEAD
TO METRO CRUISE

The 28th Street Metro Cruise, a two-day event held every August, began in 2005 when the Wyoming-Kentwood Chamber of Commerce was looking for a fun way to increase business along the 28th Street corridor. Over the years it has grown and now attracts participants across the state and across the country. About 15,000 car lovers show their vehicles each year, with about 250,000 attendees joining the fun of related activities, including car auctions, classic antique car shows, swap meets, entertainment stages, sock hops, and pin-up girl competitions, to name a few.

28thstreetmetrocruise.com

TIP

With that many people seeking nourishment, it's not surprising that a Food Truck Festival is part of the fun.

75

SPEND A DAY
DOWN ON THE FARM

Take a nostalgic trip to enjoy the pleasures of the family farm and to make new memories with the family. Family farms in the Grand Rapids area offer the chance to get out into the fresh air, pick fresh fruit, learn a bit about farming, and enjoy seasonal events.

The entire family will have fun at Robinette's Apple Haus & Winery, which is open year round. The busiest season is fall, when people can pick apples or visit the Apple Haus to purchase pre-picked apples and fresh apple cider from the cidery. This is a family destination where the family can explore the corn maze, enjoy a hayride pulled by Belgian horses, explore the scenic trails, pick out a pumpkin, and more. Adults age twenty-one and over can enjoy tasting locally made wines and hard ciders at the winery.

Post Family Farm is a family-run farm that hosts a fall festival, bonfires, and special events. Take the family to their popular fall festival, which offers horse-drawn wagon rides, hayrides to the U-Pick pumpkin patch, a corn maze, outdoor kiddie corral, games, and more.

Robinette's Apple Haus & Winery, 3142 4 Mile Rd. NE, (616) 361-5567
robinettes.com

Post Family Farm, 5081 Bauer Rd., Hudsonville, (616) 669-1964
postfamilyfarm.com

GO GHOST HUNTING
IN HAUNTED PLACES

Whether or not you believe in ghosts, a ghost hunting tour can be an interesting experience that includes storytelling about the history and folklore of the area. The Ghosts of Grand Rapids Tours are conducted by Robert and Nicole Du Shane and Julie Rathsack, authors of the book *Ghosts of Grand Rapids Tour*.

The tour guides tell the stories of paranormal happenings in historic buildings, including the AT&T Building, the Pantlind Hotel, the Ashton Building, and many other haunted locations. There are three different walking tour routes, as well as a bus tour. Tours, which run from summer through Halloween, start at the front steps of the Grand Rapids Library.

Ghosts of Grand Rapids Tours, (833) 472-7264
paranormalmichigan.com

Grand Rapids Public Library, 111 Library St. NE

TIP

Grand Rapids Running Tours offers a tour of the historic Fulton Street Graveyard all year long, but it is most popular in October. The running tours meet at the lobby of the JW Marriott. There are also walking tours that meet at the Fulton Street Cemetery. Check their website for their other tours, including America's Furniture City; Architecture of Downtown Grand Rapids; Athletes, Astronauts & All-Stars; Firehouse Fun; and others.

grandrapidsrunningtours.com

77

TOUR THE HISTORIC AMWAY GRAND HOTEL

FOR A GLIMPSE INTO OLD-FASHIONED ELEGANCE

The historic Amway Grand Plaza Hotel was originally Sweet's Hotel. J. Boyd Pantlind bought it in 1913 and renamed it the Pantlind, not for himself but for his beloved uncle. It was considered one of the top ten hotels in America. In 1979 the hotel was again sold, this time to the Amway Corporation located in Ada. The hotel was refurbished and reopened in 1981 as the Amway Grand Hotel. The attached twenty-nine-story glass tower was once the tallest skyscraper in Grand Rapids and offers spectacular views of the Grand River, the bridges, and the city. Guests can experience Four-Diamond comfort and amenities, including a hotel swimming pool, health spa, and a variety of restaurants. Dine at The Kitchen at Wolfgang Puck, Ruth's Chris Steak House, the Lumber Baron Bar, and the casual GP Sports Pub.

The downtown landmark was named the best hotel over 400 rooms by Historic Hotels of America in 2017, so visit the hotel to see the opulent décor in the lobby of this Beaux Arts architecture. The Pantlind Hotel section features the world's largest gold-leaf ceiling, so make sure to look up to see the spectacular gilded ceiling.

The Amway Grand Plaza Hotel is now in the Curio Collection by Hilton.

187 Monroe Ave. NE, (616) 774-2000

TIP

The Amway Grand Plaza Hotel is conveniently located downtown, so it is a great base for visitors attending conventions and entertainment in the city. The DeVos Place Convention Center is connected via the Grand River Promenade to the DeVos Place Convention Center, and the Van Andel Arena is within walking distance from the hotel.

TRACE YOUR ROOTS
AT THE GRAND RAPIDS PUBLIC LIBRARY

If you're interested in genealogy or local history, begin your search on the 4th floor of the Grand Rapids Public Library. Here you will find nearly five hundred special collections of images, diaries, letters, ephemera, maps, and postcards to browse. There is also an extensive clipping file, along with vertical files, newspapers on microfiche, city directories, and much more. The staff are knowledgeable, approachable, and eager to help.

The main library is in a lovely old building downtown with a modern addition providing much-needed space. The oldest part of the building was a gift from Martin A. Ryerson, a Grand Rapids native and grandson of Antoine Campau, the brother of city founder, Louis Campau.

Seven branches are strategically located around the city. Together they provide programs, author readings, computer classes, activities for children and teens, and books, books, books!

111 Library St. NE, (616) 988-5400
grpl.org

79

CELEBRATE THE ARTS
DURING ARTPRIZE

Celebrate the arts by exploring the art installations around the city during ArtPrize, which is free and open to the public. ArtPrize is a big-ticket art event that awards more than $500,000 to winning artists and attracts over 500,000 visitors.

Art is exhibited throughout Grand Rapids for three weeks in the fall. Visitors can find the installations at the bridges, museums, public parks, bars, restaurants, hotels, theaters, office spaces, auto body shops, laundromats, and in vacant storefronts.

The installations bring the creativity artists from around the world to Grand Rapids, sharing their visions and new ideas. This is an excellent opportunity to expand your horizons and look at life and art from a unique point of view.

ArtPrize has been an annual event for several years, but it has been changed to a biennial event, so it will be held every two years. On alternate years there will be a project event featuring commissioned artists. The new art event will still be a large-scale event held at multiple sites, so visitors should plan to explore the exciting art installations while the programs run in September and October, whether it be ArtPrize or a Project 1 art event.

artprize.org

GRAND RAPIDS
CHILDREN'S MUSEUM

Instead of being a chore, learning is fun when young minds are developed by in the playful atmosphere at the Grand Rapids Children's Museum. Take the kids to have fun while exploring exhibits and participating in special events. Kids enjoy big city fun at the kid-sized "Little GR!," which features downsized versions of area businesses, especially for little ones. The new "Think Tank" exhibit expands on the popular "Imagination Playground," with pipe play and a giant Rigamajig set. Fun exhibits include beehives, bubbles, farm fun, fort fun, and other ways to play and stimulate the imagination and encourage exploration.

11 Sheldon Ave. NE, (616) 235-4726
grcm.org

LEARN ABOUT
AFRICAN AMERICAN CULTURE

The Grand Rapids African American Museum & Archives (GRAAMA) preserves the history passed down through generations of storytellers. Oral history and the keeping of history and family traditions was a job of the men of African tribes. When Africans were brought to the Americas, the duty of storytelling shifted to womenfolk, a grandmother, granny, grandma, nana, or GRAAMA. In describing their mission and acronym, they say "Always listen to your GRAAMA."

Visit GRAAMA to learn about African American history and culture and to honor the people of the community. The museum is located one block east of Rosa Parks Circle, a Grand Rapids landmark honoring the famed Civil Rights pioneer.

GRAAMA, 87 Monroe Center St., (616) 540-2943
graama.org

GET THE THREE-DAY CULTURE PASS
AND EXPLORE

Culture Pass GR offers an abundance of art and culture over a three-day period. For $24 you get general admission to some of the best attractions in the city, including the Gerald R. Ford Presidential Museum, Grand Rapids African American Museum and Archives, Grand Rapids Art Museum, Grand Rapids Children's Museum, Grand Rapids Public Museum, John Ball Zoo, and the Urban Institute for Contemporary Arts. The pass also offers discounts at some the popular entertainment venues around town.

If you are able to visit multiple attractions over a three-day period you can save money on admission while seeing the plethora of culture in the city. The pass includes exclusive discounts to the Actors' Theatre, Broadway Grand Rapids, Circle Theatre, Civic Theatre, DeVos Performance Hall, The Dinner Detective, Grand Rapids Ballet, Opera Grand Rapids, and River City Improv.

Purchase the Culture Pass and it will be immediately transferred to your phone and activated when you visit the first attraction. To get your Culture Pass, see the website at culturepass.experiencegr.com

TIP

Some attractions, such as the Grand Rapids Art Museum, offer free admission on certain days. Many of the cultural attractions in the city offer free admission during ArtPrize. Check the schedules of the attractions you are most interested in to see if they have any free days that fit into your schedule.

The Shops at MoDiv serve as an in incubator for retail entrepreneurs.
Photo Credit, The Shops at MoDiv

SHOPPING AND FASHION

FIND WHAT YOU NEED
AT DOWNTOWN BOUTIQUES

Of course Grand Rapids has malls. Every city does. There's RiverTown Crossings in Grandville, Woodland Mall on 28th Street, and a Tanger Outlet Mall in Byron Center. Downtown was once a thriving retail center, with Steketee's and Herpolshimer's department stores among the mix. They're both long gone, but shopping still exists when you don't want to follow the pack. Check out the boutiques found in the Amway Grand Plaza Hotel and the MoDiv (Monroe Street and Division Avenue). Within the hotel you'll find Emmanuel and Emmanuel Too for women. Men will find everything they need at the Plaza Men's Shop. There is also Essentials Gift Shop for souvenirs, books, and other odds and ends, along with Zeller's Party Store.

MoDiv is an ever-changing eclectic mix housed in what is called a small business incubator. Shop owners can test the market in a small venue before expanding to larger, more expensive locations. As of late 2018, boutiques included Dear Prudence, Humanity, Jagger Madison, and Off the Cuff.

Amway Grand Plaza, 187 Monroe Ave. NE

MoDiv, 40 Monroe Ave. NE

GO NUTS
AT KOEZE'S

Long before shopping and sourcing local was in vogue, area residents flocked to Koeze's for holiday gifts or their own favorite munchies. Koeze products are also popular as corporate gifts. In 1910, Sibelle Koeze founded Koeze's wholesale grocery business to sell eggs, butter, and produce to area grocers. The company is still family owned and operated and has long since switched to gourmet nuts and peanut butter, along with chocolates and other candies. It would be hard to find anyone who doesn't like the cashews and the turtles. The peanut butter is the old-fashioned kind in which the oil rises to the top and needs stirring. Yum!

2555 Burlington Ave. SW, Wyoming, (616) 724-2620
koeze.com

TIP
There is a second retail store at 1971 E. Beltline Ave. NE.

SHOP FOR DUTCH TREATS
AT THE DUTCH STORE

If you are among the Dutch of the area, the VanderVeen's Dutch Store is the place to go. Here you'll find a dazzling array of Delft china, lace, wooden shoes, holiday ornaments, household items, and more. Even if the Netherlands is not the homeland of your ancestors, the store is still a good source of Dutch treats, some of which are hard to find anywhere else. Imported grocery brands include Droste chocolates, Koopman mixes to make pofferties (small pancakes) and Stroopwafel (cake), de Ruyter speculaas (spiced cookies in the shape of windmills), Honig soups, Venco and Katja drops (licorice candies), and Wilhelmina mints. Don't overlook the deli case filled with Gouda, Edam, and other cheeses, along with mettwurst and pigs in blankets. One popular Dutch treat is banket, a scrumptious dessert made with almond paste. If you prefer, you can buy the almond paste and make your own.

28th St. SW, Wyoming, (800) 813-9538
thedutchstore.com

TIP

The Dutch are not the only ones catering to those of other cultures. Russo's on 29th St. is the go-to for anything Italian. There are also numerous Hispanic, Asian, and other markets in which to find the goods representing the immigrant's homeland. Or anyone else seeking to add a bit of the exotic to their everyday diet.

86

LET GEORGIE
DRESS YOU

No longer looked down upon, consignment shopping is now considered smart shopping whether you need a special occasion outfit that you may never wear again, or you simply want to refresh your wardrobe with great finds at a reasonable price. For many Grand Rapids area women, the best of the best is Georgie's Consignment Shop in Ada. The shop is special for several reasons, one of which is that it has been going strong for thirty-five years. Another is that items are kept in the shop for only sixty days and are marked down as the deadline approaches. That means new merchandise is continually being brought in. Also, if you are looking for something you would love to have but that is totally outside of your budget, you just might find it in the Designer Room. This is where Burberry, Prada, and Chanel among other top, but pricey, designer pieces can be found.

7504 Thornapple River Dr., Ada, (616) 676-1869
georgiesconsignment.com

TIP

There are other clothing consignment shops around the area, including LBD Exchange, Blooming Deal, Rosie's Closet, and Denym. And clothing isn't the only thing that's consigned. If your home décor needs a little tweak or even a major overhaul, check out the Furniture City Consignment Store.

3555 Lake Eastbrook Blvd. SE, (616) 940-4123
furniturecityconsignment.com

FIND SOMETHING OLD
AND WONDERFUL

For one-stop antique shopping look no further than the 400 block of Century Avenue. The old Sligh Furniture factory now houses three large antique malls: Warehouse One, Lost and Found Treasures of Old and New, and Century Antiques. Combined they boast more than six hundred vendors, and whatever you collect or happen to be looking for, you'll likely find it here—from armoires to zithers. You might even find a piece of Sligh furniture. But probably not at Lost and Found Treasures of Old and New, where the specialty is mid-century modern. Here's where to search for Herman Miller, including Eames chairs and marshmallow sofas, Heywood Wakefield, and the like.

Warehouse One, 449 Century Ave. SW, (616) 235-9292
warehouseone@aol.com

Lost and Found Treasures of Old and New
445 Century Ave. SW, (616) 732-3401
treasuresoflostandfound.com

Century Antiques, 445 Century Ave. SW, (616) 233-4000
centurystreetantiques.com

Another great spot for antique hunting is Eastown Antiques in the Eastown neighborhood. The collection is large and eclectic, and the staff is helpful.

1515 Lake Dr. SE, (616) 776-1076
eastownantiques.com

START, OR ADD TO, AN ANTIQUARIAN BOOK COLLECTION

Argos owner Jim Bleeker has an extensive inventory. Along with the rare and out-of-print collectible antiquarian books, he has new releases and a huge supply of gently used and affordable reads. Among those are classics, fiction, history, sports, children's, sci-fi, fantasy, graphic, comics, local authors, and much, much more. Some of the vintage paperbacks are priced as low as fifty cents. Those with an interest in Michigan history will find books, posters from the Furniture City days, high school yearbooks, Calvin and other local college yearbooks, church directories, photos, and ephemera. Bleeker is a man who knows and loves books and is eager to share his knowledge. Don't plan to dash in and out, as this is a place that grabs you as soon as you walk in the door.

1405 Robinson Rd. SE, (616) 454-0111
argosbooks.com

TIP

Redux is right around the corner on Lake Drive, and also has an eclectic mix. Along with two of the ubiquitous Barnes and Noble bookstores, the Grand Rapids area also boasts three independent booksellers: Schuler's and Brick and Mortar in the city, and Epilogue in suburban Rockford. Get to know them all. Your inner bookworm will thank you.

TICKLE YOUR TASTE BUDS
AT THE DOWNTOWN MARKET

The Downtown Market has been referred to as a delicious destination and rightly so. Twenty purveyors of fine foods will tempt you. The Fish Lads offer fresh seafood flown in daily and a raw bar with a limited eat-in menu. Check out the butcher shop Carvers, Grand Rapids' finest meats. A local favorite, and likely to become yours too, is Sweetie-licious Bake Shoppe for award-winning pies, quiche, cupcakes, and cookies. If you're looking for bread instead of sweets, you'll find it at Field and Fire Bakery. For specialized selections, there is Apertivo, Old World Olive Company, Spice Merchants, Making Thyme Kitchen, Malamiah Juice Bar, Rak Thai, Blue Spoon Pasta Studio, Madcap Coffee, Dorothy and Tony's Gourmet Popcorn, Relish Green Grocer, Sushi Market, and Love's Ice Cream. Some serve food to be consumed on the premises. Other restaurant options include Rocket Pies (pizza), Social Kitchen and Bar, Tacos El Cunado, and Slow's Bar B-Q.

435 Ionia Ave. SW, (616) 805-5308
downtownmarket.com

FIND JUST-PICKED PRODUCE

AT THE FULTON STREET FARMERS MARKET

Enjoy summer with vine-ripened tomatoes still warm from the sun. Or savor juicy melons of all types, Michigan peaches, and blueberries. Buy lettuce and other salad makings fresh from the farm instead of supermarket aisles. Michigan summers are short, so feast while you can. The produce, though reason enough to go, is only part of the goodies you can find. Fresh baked breads and desserts. Artisan cheeses. Farm-fresh meat. Jerky. Fresh flowers. Ready-to-eat hotdogs. Gourmet popcorn. Ice cream. Coffee. It isn't just your taste buds that will be tempted, there are also vendors selling hand-crafted items such as soaps, mittens, home décor, jams and jellies, wreaths and dried flower arrangements, and more. The market is open Tuesday, Wednesday, Friday, and Saturday, from early May through late December. Obviously you won't find garden fresh produce when the season is over, but stop and check out the gift, craft, and holiday items that include Christmas trees. A heated winter market is open Saturdays from January through April.

1145 Fulton St. E, (616) 454-4118
fultonstreetmarket.org

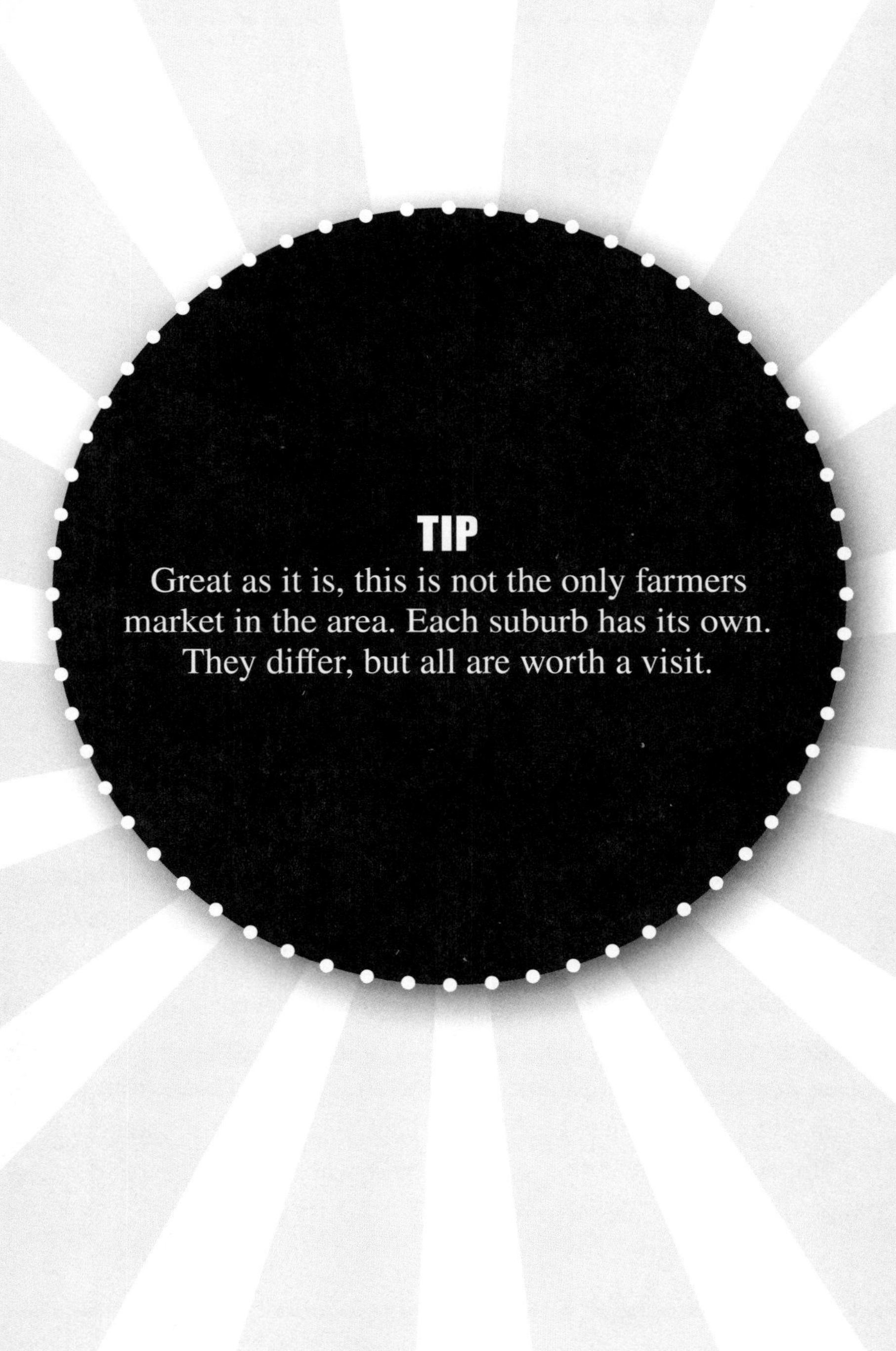
TIP
Great as it is, this is not the only farmers market in the area. Each suburb has its own. They differ, but all are worth a visit.

91

EXPLORE EAST GRAND RAPIDS
FOR AN ECLECTIC SHOPPING MIX

Nestled on Reed's Lake, East Grand Rapids is home to an impressive array of boutiques and dining. One-of-a-kind shops here include Blackbird East for gifts and clothing for both men and women; Dear Prudence; Bella's Furs; Baby Mine, featuring everything you could wish for in terms of clothing and toys for the little ones in your life. Another venue not to miss is the Breton Village Mall where you'll find Talbot's, Orvis, and Anthropologie among the chains, and one-of-a-kind boutiques like Scout and Molly's for women's clothing and accessories. If you need lunch or breakfast while shopping at Breton Village, visit the Omelette Shop. The raspberry muffins will make you glad you did.

Ramona Park, which once drew crowds for its shows and amusements, is long gone with the exception of Rose's on Reed's Lake, a popcorn shop in its amusement park days and now a charming lakefront restaurant. There you'll receive a small cup of popcorn instead of an after-dinner mint, as a nod to its past. End your East Grand Rapids day with an ice cream cone from the Jersey Junction, founded in 1963 by Chris Van Allsburg, mother of a famed children's writer and illustrator who is a former resident and also named Chris Van Allsburg.

SATISFY YOUR CURIOSITY

AT THE MUSEUM'S CURIOSITY SHOP

A great source of truly distinctive items can be found in the gift shops in museums and other organizations. The Grand Rapids Museum operates the Curiosity Shop. More than a whimsical name, the shop will both inspire and satisfy your curiosity, and its wares far surpass the clichéd t-shirt. Some merchandise is directly related to permanent exhibits, while some celebrate West Michigan. As traveling exhibits appear, so does the related merchandise on the shelves. Look for build-your-own biplanes, locally crafted jewelry, fossils, books, and much more. Think food items made of Michigan cherries or freeze-dried astronaut ice cream. In short, this is where you'll find those special gifts you can't find anywhere else. Don't forget to put your own name on your gift list.

TIP

If you're looking for great gifts for local residents, also consider museum memberships or season tickets to sports or entertainment venues.

93

FIND ART GALLERIES
FOR ALL TASTES

Even before ArtPrize put Grand Rapids on the radar, the city appreciated its art and artists. Flourishing galleries have long been part of the local scene. Since 1999, MercuryHead Gallery has provided original local art along with custom framing, unique gifts, jewelry, Celtic items, and contemporary furniture. The LaFontsee Gallery represents more than seventy contemporary artists, jewelry makers, and other crafters, including Carl Forslund, Toni Swarthout, Christy DeHoog, and Jennifer McCurdy. They operate a second gallery in Douglas.

MercuryHead Gallery, 962 Fulton St. E, (616) 456-6022
mercuryheadgallery.com

LaFontsee Gallery, 833 Lake Dr. SE, (616) 451-9820
lafontsee.us/community

TIP

The next local star might now be a student at the Kendall College of Art and Design in downtown Grand Rapids. Check out their displays. Other galleries and displays can be found at the Calvin College Center Art Gallery and the Urban Institute of Contemporary Art.

94

SHOP THE LATEST AND GREATEST
AT AN EXPOSITION OR TRADE SHOW

A favorite is the three-day Women's Expo held annually in March. Thousands of shoppers storm DeVos Place to check out the 350-plus exhibitors displaying wares of interest to women. These include health, beauty, clothing, jewelry, home, food, and some that are just plain fun. Demonstrations, seminars, presentations and entertainment add up to an extravaganza not to be missed. Check out all the newest bells and whistles as well as the tried and true. It's all here and all designed to make her heart beat faster.

TIP

Whatever your passion, there is likely a show promoting it. The best of the best are held at DeVos Place or the Deltaplex Arena, and include annual home and garden shows, bridal shows, boat shows, car shows, RV shows, fishing shows, comic book shows, antiques shows . . . You get the idea.

DeVos Place, 303 Monroe Ave. NW, (616) 742-6500
devosplace.org

Deltaplex Arena, 2500 Turner Ave. NW, (616) 364-9000
deltaplex.com

Also check the Experience Grand Rapids website
for more information, experiencegr.com

95

BEAUTIFY YOUR LANDSCAPE

INDOORS AND OUTDOORS AT FLOWERLAND

There's nothing like flowers and green plants to beautify the landscape and freshen the air—indoors and out. Gardens bloom around the region during the warm weather months, so join the people who take pride in their yards by adding a garden to your landscape.

Don't have a yard? Decorate your home or apartment by placing attractive green plants inside, where you can enjoy them year-round.

Flowerland is a Grand Rapids area garden center with three locations to offer everything you need to plant a garden. You can also purchase cut flowers to decorate your home or to give as a gift for a special occasion. Whether you dream of planting a rose garden, spring bulbs, shrubs, put pots on the porch, or any other type of garden, you can find the supplies and advice to make it happen at Flowerland.

Flowerland Alpine, 3801 Alpine Ave. NW, Comstock Park, (616) 784-0542
myflowerland.com

Flowerland Wyoming, 765 28th St. SW, Wyoming, (616) 532-5934

Flowerland Kentwood, 4321 28th St. SE, Kentwood, (616) 942-5321

TIP

Learn great gardening tips by tuning in to the Flowerland radio show featuring CEO Rick Vuyst, a local personality who loves his work and enthusiastically shares his knowledge. You can learn about timely gardening topics a from a Greenthumb expert on his long-running weekly radio show on NewsRadioWOOD 1300 and 106.9 FM on Saturday mornings. He is known for agricultural puns, which he shares in his book about life and gardening, titled *I Just Wet My Plants*, and his website thankyouverymulch.

SHOP TRENDY EAST HILLS
AND SAVE PLANET EARTH

The portion of the East Hills neighborhood where Lake, Diamond, and Cherry streets converge is an area of hip boutiques and other shops easily explored on foot. The one word you hear describing most of the clothing shops is "sustainable." Clothing Matters urges you to "feel good in what you wear" and offers items made of organic cotton and hemp. All products adhere to Fair Trade standards. A similar philosophy will be found at the Hopscotch Children's Store, with clothing for infants through size 12. They also stock Smart Bottoms cloth diapers, green toys, books, and more, with a preference for Michigan-made items. Swirls is yet another sustainable clothing boutique selling both men's and women's clothing to appeal to a socially responsible clientele. Rock Paper Scissors Consignment Boutique offers gently worn women's clothing and accessories. Also, visit the Y T Galleria for "unparalleled finds with unmistakable character," a tall order, but one they manage to fill. You'll find an eclectic mix of apparel, accessories, jewelry, pottery, and art.

Hunt and Gather offers interior decorating services and maintains a carefully curated stock of everything you need to create a vintage-modern aesthetic sustainable environment. Heartwood Antiques is a small shop specializing in Mission-style furniture and accessories and Grand Rapids–made furniture. The owner delights in telling you the history of a piece when known. The LaFontsee Gallery is also in this neighborhood.

97

INDULGE YOUR SWEET TOOTH
WITH DECADENT CHOCOLATE

Sweetland Candies has been offering treats to satisfy the sweet tooth since 1919. The confectionery is now in its fourth generation of expert candy makers, offering fine locally made chocolates and sweets.

Shop at Sweetland Candies for boxed chocolates for holiday gift giving and special treats for loved ones. Their fine chocolates include seafoam, turtles, caramels, mints, creams, and many more. They also offer gourmet nuts and other treats.

Relatively new to the scene is Mokaya, offering gourmet artisan chocolates, desserts, and drinks. The name Mokaya is a tribute to an ancient Mesoamerican culture. The Mokaya people created a drink from cacao. Mokaya's chocolatier uses fair trade cocoa beans from Latin America to create its chocolate treats.

Shop at Mokaya to experience exquisite chocolate combinations and flavors, artfully presented to delight the senses. Try the rich assortment of chocolate confections, beverages, pastries, and ice cream.

Sweetland Candies, 5170 Plainfield Ave. NE, (616) 363-3444
sweetlandcandies.com

Sweetland Candies, 9 North Main St. NE, Rockford, (616) 884-0021

Mokaya, 638 Wealthy St. SE, (616) 551-1925
mokayagr.com

98

TREAT YOURSELF TO ICE CREAM

While you are out shopping or seeing the sights in town, a refreshing ice cream treat can be a great pick-me-up. Treat yourself to locally made ice cream from one of the popular ice cream parlors around the city.

Jersey Junction, in Gaslight Village, is an old-fashioned ice cream parlor that was established by Doris "Chris" Van Allsburg in 1963. The parlor is decorated with pictures from Ramona Park, a popular amusement park that was once at the site. The owner's son is author Chris Van Allsburg, who wrote the best-selling children's book *Polar Express,* which was made into the movie starring Tom Hanks. Two models of the Polar Express are displayed at the shop. Jersey Junction serves several flavors of ice cream made by Hudsonville Ice Cream.

Love's Ice Cream & Chocolate and Furniture City Creamery hand craft ice cream in small batches on the premises. Visitors can enjoy freshly made creamy treats in a variety of flavors. Visit the ice cream parlors for a special treat.

Jersey Junction, 652 Croswell Ave. SE, (616) 458-4107
jerseyjunction.com

Love's Ice Cream & Chocolate, 435 Ionia Ave. SW, stall 106
(616) 965-1054, lovesicecream.com

Furniture City Creamery, 958 Cherry St.. SE, (616) 920-0752
furniturecitycreamery.com

99

EAT PIE FIRST
AT SWEETIE-LICIOUS

Step into a nostalgic bakery for treats, pies, and baked goods made from family recipes. Sweetie-licious owner Linda Hundt wrote about learning the art of pie making from her mother, aunts, and grandmother in her book *Sweetie-licious Pies: Eat Pie, Love Life*. The pies have been shown on *The Today Show*, *Food and Wine*, and The Food Network. The pies are featured nationally in Williams Sonoma.

You can enjoy the homey ambience where love, tradition, and people are celebrated through good comfort food and homemade pies and other baked goods. The pies and baked goods are made from scratch and feature handmade fillings. There are over fifty varieties of pie, although some flavors are seasonal so are not available year-round. The delicious offerings include Tom's Cherry Cherry Berry Berry, Cherry Blueberry Raspberry, Key Lime Raspberry, Raspberry Cream, and many more.

The café serves sandwiches, quiches, salads, and soups. Stop in for a bite to eat but save room for pie, or better yet, eat pie first. Then take some pie home to share with loved ones.

Downtown Market, 435 Ionia Ave. SW, (616) 259-7005
sweetie-licious.com

108 North Bridge St., DeWitt, (517) 669-9300

TIP

You can also find great pies at Grand Traverse Pie Company, with area shops located in Norton Shores and Kentwood. Their café menu offers quiches, pot pies, sandwiches, salads, soups, and more. Take home their top-selling Grand Traverse Cherry Crumb Pie, Cherry Ganache Pie, or one (or more) of their many other delicious pies.

3224 28th St. SE, Kentwood, (616) 977-7600
gtpie.com

Pheasant Run Plaza, 5817 Harvey St.
Norton Shores, (231) 799-3399

BUY A DO-IT-YOURSELF PAINTING
AT BRUSH STUDIOS

Looking for something new and different? For a fun night out and an original (by you) painting to deck your hall, reserve your spot at Brush Studios. No experience is required. Thirty to thirty-five dollars buys you a 16 x 20-inch canvas and the use of acrylic paint, brushes, an easel, and an apron. Each class features a painting that an artist will guide you through replicating step by step. All this is done in a laid-back social setting with wine and beer available for purchase. Raise your glass. Wield your paintbrush. Take home a piece of art that will amaze you. Attend a scheduled class or arrange a private group event. Great for corporate team-building workshops, girls' night out, bachelorette parties, or any other celebrations you can think of.

50 Louis St. NW, (616) 570-0682
brushgr.com

TIP

Cat lovers can have the same experience at the Happy Cat Café with a cat on their lap. The shelter is available for private parties and the adoptable kitties are adorable.

477 S. Division Ave., (616) 202-4750
happycatcompany.com

Photo credit: Christine Nyholm

SUGGESTED ITINERARIES

GET ACTIVE

LET THEM ENTERTAIN YOU

FUN FOR THE WHOLE FAMILY

RECIPE FOR ROMANCE

Gerald R. Ford Presidential Museum.
Photo credit: Christine Nyholm

ACTIVITIES
BY SEASON

SPRING

SUMMER

FALL

WINTER

Amway Grand Plaza Hotel
Photo credit: Christine Nyholm

INDEX

Cottage Bar. Photo credit: Christine Nyholm

Franky the Swimming Pig and Roxy the River Rascal
Photo credit: West Michigan Whitecaps